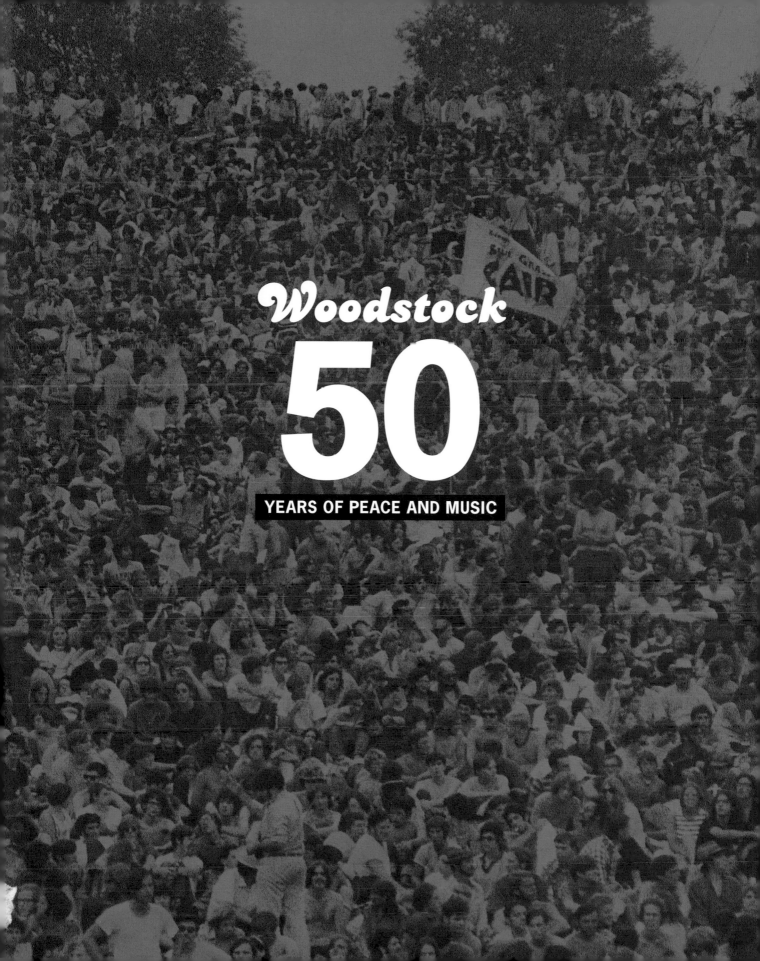

An Imagine Book
Published by Charlesbridge
85 Main Street
Watertown, MA 02472
(617) 926-0329
www.imaginebooks.net

Library of Congress Cataloging-in-Publication data available upon request

ISBN 978-1-62354-531-4 (reinforced for library use)
ISBN 978-1-63289-222-5 (ebook)
ISBN 978-1-63289-223-2 (ebook pdf)

Printed in China
(hc) 10 9 8 7 6 5 4 3 2 1

Jacket and Book Design by Lynne Yeamans
Photo research by Julie Tesser
Project supervision by Karen Matsu Greenberg

Principal Photography © Amalie R. Rothschild

The author has made every effort to ensure the accuracy of the information within this
book was correct at time of publication. The author does not assume and hereby disclaims
any liability to any party for any loss, damage, or disruption caused by errors or omissions,
whether such errors or omissions result from accident, negligence, or any other cause.

Due to the nature of audience participation, model releases are not applicable.

LISTEN TO THE ARTISTS WHO PERFORMED AT WOODSTOCK. EACH PLAYLIST
PRESENTS THE ARTISTS IN THE ORDER IN WHICH THEY PLAYED.

Due to licensing issues beyond our control, some artists don't appear in every
streaming service catalog, and the availability of certain songs changes frequently.
Some artists will not always appear on these playlists, and others that are there
today may not be there tomorrow.

WoodstockDayOneSampler.com

WoodstockDayTwoSampler.com

WoodstockDayThreeSampler.com

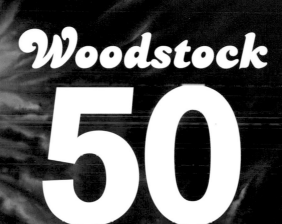

Woodstock
50
YEARS OF PEACE AND MUSIC

DANIEL BUKSZPAN

Foreword by Melanie
Principal Photography by Amalie R. Rothschild

imagine!

Contents

Foreword

When I went onstage at Woodstock, I was a virtual unknown. Maybe a small percent of the people in that audience had heard my song, "Beautiful People," because disc jockeys like Rosko in New York played it a lot, but otherwise I was a stranger.

My producer, Peter Schekeryk, who later became my husband, arranged for me to play there, and I truly had no clue what it was or how important it was. I was living in England, where I was working on a film score and recording in a studio next to where the Rolling Stones were. Sometimes the Small Faces would show up at the clubs where I played to perform a few songs. My life in England seemed like it was really going somewhere, so why would I want to leave all that behind just to play one concert?

But Peter said, "No, no, you go," and I did.

My mother picked me up at the airport, and the next day, we drove up to do this thing. When we got to the motel near the festival grounds, I saw that it was not going to be a casual picnic in the park like I thought. It was for sure bigger than what I was doing in England.

The parking lot was filled with media trucks from one end to the other, and I didn't have any great desire to be part of that whole thing. But they put me in a helicopter and I got there when Richie Havens was singing. I flew over the field, and I'd never seen a stage this big. It was a football field–sized stage.

I was familiar with Richie Havens because I hung around Greenwich Village a lot, and he was a big deal there. By the time I got to my tent, he was playing "Freedom," and I could tell that there was terror in his voice. Almost anybody would be terrified playing to a crowd that size.

When it was my turn to play, I walked on a wobbly bridge to get to the stage, and it felt like I was walking the plank.

I don't think I had a set list, and if I did, it was something I had done in England weeks before. I sang "Beautiful People," and that was the only song that I was armed with that was slightly familiar to anybody there.

I resonated. These were my people.

I walked onstage an unknown person with slight industry buzz, and I walked offstage a celebrity. The next day, people were contacting me to do all sorts of things. I got a call to do a panel show with anthropologists, and I hadn't done any television shows before.

Woodstock made me famous, and it was a catalyst for my career, but I always knew that Woodstock wasn't really about me or any other performer. It was really more about this coming together and showing a kindred spirit. It was a gathering. And people still want to be a part of that gathering, whether they were there or not.

It reminded me of the movie *Close Encounters of the Third Kind*, where Richard Dreyfus's character is building this thing. He doesn't know what it is or why he's doing it, but he knows he has to go to a certain place at a certain time, and so do hundreds of other people, who also don't know why they're going there… they just know that they have to.

Woodstock was the same. It pulled people, and it still pulls people. You could say that there was something of a pilgrimage about it, and the fact that we're still here talking about it fifty years later means that the people who made that pilgrimage were right, even if they weren't sure what it meant at the time.

The music business has changed a lot since then. People who cared about music were at the head of A&R, not people who were just good at going to cocktail parties. But it

wasn't long before the record company that I was with got taken over by lawyers. It was really the beginning of the corporate music business.

Even so, Woodstock is still a big part of what I do every day. I'm on tour right now as I write this, and people are still bringing candles to light at my shows whenever I perform "Lay Down (Candles in the Rain)," the song I wrote after I played there. So even though the music industry has changed, people have changed, and the world has changed, Woodstock is still pulling people in, like it did that weekend in August.

I don't know how my life would have gone if I had stayed in England instead of performing at Woodstock, or if Peter hadn't talked me into it, or if my mother hadn't driven me there. But I'm so glad that they did, and I'm so glad that I went. And I'm just so grateful that I got to be a part of it.

—MELANIE

Introduction

There's a clichéd saying that if you can remember Woodstock, then you weren't really there.

It isn't true. In researching this book, I interviewed dozens of people who were there, and all of them remember it, vividly and with great affection.

They remember the rain on their skin. They remember the smell of pot smoke and body odor. They remember the stranger who shared his lump of brown rice with them, even if they have forgotten his name. They remember the mud between their toes. They remember not having a ride home.

They remember it all, because you don't forget things like that. You don't forget anything that happened when you were eighteen, and feeling that mixture of anxiety and exhilaration that's only possible at that age.

As for me, I wasn't there. In fact, I wasn't even born yet. I was born six weeks later, on October 1, 1969, but I certainly heard a lot about it, mostly from people who weren't there either.

I heard about it from teachers, when they wanted to make a point about moral decline. I heard about it from peers, who were punks or goths, and who used the word "Woodstock" pejoratively, to suggest a naïve utopianism for which they had no respect.

None of these people were talking about an event. They were talking about something they didn't like and slapping a festival's name on it, to lend credibility to their grousing. They weren't talking about something that real people had experienced.

In researching this book, I interviewed people who were in the audience that weekend. I also talked to members of the technical crew, promoters, performers, and anyone else who was there and wanted to talk about it.

Most of what I believed to be true was wrong, and a lot had happened that I never knew about. These people described extremely uncomfortable conditions, which they endured in order to hear the music they loved.

They sat shoulder to shoulder with complete strangers, in an impromptu society with an unspoken social contract that everyone understood. Those things get lost in the hagiography, and they deserve to be recognized.

This sign advertises the Woodstock festival at its original location in Wallkill, New York.

Much of the coverage of Woodstock at the time focused on the lack of amenities and general unpleasantness. All of that is true, and understandably, it's led many people to ask about Woodstock, "What went wrong?"

This is the wrong question. The Altamont Speedway Free Festival, which was marred by violence and death, took place only four months later, and it showed that many gatherings descend into chaos. Sporting events, with enough food and seating for everyone, have descended into riots, with overturned cars, smashed windows, and fires, even when the home team wins.

Given the conditions that the Woodstock audience endured, why didn't the same thing happen? Why didn't it turn ugly?

The real question to ask, really, is not "What went wrong?" It's "What went right?"

Dan Mouer, a Vietnam veteran and author of the book *Warbaby: Talking About My Generation*, worked in the underground press and covered Woodstock. He described conditions that don't come through on the soundtrack album.

"Crowded. No food. Practically no toilets," he said. "We all slept on the ground in the rain. And mud. Lots of mud."

He went home early, but he was there long enough to see why Woodstock didn't go down in history as The Catskill Mountains Humanitarian Crisis.

"It was a bit of a nightmare, but folks shared, helped each other, made the best of it," he said. "It was miserably uncomfortable, but most everyone seems to have enjoyed it...loved it, even."

Promoter Joel Rosenman, one of the three surviving members of the Woodstock Ventures organization that produced the festival, credited the audience with the refusal to let Woodstock go down in history as a catastrophe.

> *It was a bit of a nightmare, but folks shared, helped each other, made the best of it. It was miserably uncomfortable, but most everyone seems to have enjoyed it...loved it, even.*
>
> —DAN MOUER

"It's clear if you think about it for more than fifteen minutes, the real hero of Woodstock is the audience," he said. "They endured a lot, and in the words of Max Yasgur, they showed the world that *Homo sapiens* is not necessarily a lethal mutation. It's actually got these very fine instincts for taking care of each other, loving one another, supporting one another, and that was all in the audience."

Unless a specific outside source is cited in the text or in the bibliography, this book is based entirely on interviews with people who were at Woodstock, whether they were audience members, band members, crew members, or promoters.

For that reason, you'll see contradictory information about certain things. Rosenman referred to this as "the *Rashomon* effect," after the Akira Kurosawa movie in which different people remember one event in different ways. The viewer comes away believing that despite the contradictions, nobody is lying.

I believe the same thing happened here. There were many cases where one person's account of an event differed from another's, sometimes to the degree that one of them had to be wrong. In those cases, I left in both accounts, or all the accounts.

I honestly believe that everyone was telling the truth, or at least telling what they sincerely believed the truth to be. It's been a long time since August 1969, and the passage of time plays tricks on you. This was never clearer to me than when one person would recall an event, and then say to me, "I can't remember, did that happen to me or was that in the movie?"

There were people I would have loved to speak with who, sadly, aren't here anymore. The perspective of the fourth promoter, John Roberts, would have been invaluable to me, but he passed away in 2001. I was able to fill in the gaps with interviews with those who knew him, but it's not really the same thing. Still, I'm very grateful for the input of those who knew him, and who wish he was still here too.

I also wanted to give space to performers who never got the coverage that the famous

Abandoned cars stretched for miles on the way to the festival grounds. Canned Heat's roadies lifted some of them out of the way, by hand, to get the group's equipment through.

ones did. I was very pleased to hear first-person accounts from Nancy Nevins of Sweetwater and Dan Cole of Quill, who were there as much as Jimi Hendrix was. They're part of the story, they're part of Woodstock history, and their perspectives belong in this book.

Because of the time when it happened, Woodstock touches on a host of other subjects—the Vietnam War, political assassinations, general social turmoil. This book is not about any of those things, though. This book is about the immediate experience of the people who were there, when they were there.

I'm very grateful to everyone who granted interviews for sharing their time with me, as well as the photographers, archivists, historians, and other people who helped me connect

the dots. None of them had to do it, but they really wanted to, and their enthusiasm inspired me. It fueled me at times when it seemed like this was a subject that I, someone who hadn't even been born yet, had no right to talk about.

The world today feels far removed from the one in which Woodstock was possible, where more than 400,000 strangers congregated peacefully for three days. Every person responsible for it deserves recognition and deserves to be remembered.

That includes Richard Julio, who was twenty-three when he went there, and who shared his memories with me.

"Thank you for doing this," he said to me. "I'm glad you're catching us, getting this down before everybody's gone." ◆

BEGINNINGS

People, given a chance, will rise to the occasion. And in this case, you had a tremendous number of people who rose to the occasion. The Indians up in that area, the Hog Farmers, people just with other people, who shared in and worked their way through it.

—JOHN MORRIS

Michael Lang

Michael Lang booked almost every act that performed at Woodstock. Before that, he had coproduced the 1968 Miami Pop Festival, featuring performances by such artists as the Crazy World of Arthur Brown, Blue Cheer, and the Jimi Hendrix Experience.

> *We thought from day one that if we did it right, if we gave people more than they were expecting and brought them to nature, everybody would behave and show their best sides,...and that is kind of what happened.*
>
> —MICHAEL LANG

"I was sort of inspired by Monterey Pop, so we called it Miami Pop," he said.

When the festival ended, he moved to Woodstock, New York. The town was known as an artists' hub, and it was home to Bob Dylan. It held "Sound-Outs" during the summer, overnight concerts on small farms just outside town, and the concept of bringing music out into nature left a lasting impression on Lang.

"Things were turning violent in the States, and 1968 was the year of the assassination of Robert F. Kennedy and Martin Luther King, and riots around the world," he said. "We were kind of losing this dream, and so we thought, 'Let's give it one last shot, and take people out of the cities and take them out of their usual pressures and see if we could make it work on our own.'"

Despite his idealism, he knew that a large gathering of young people would present challenges.

"There was a movement afoot in the counterculture that said music should be free," he said. "The logic behind it was kind of flawed. I mean, somebody's got to pay the bands, got to pay the stage crew. Without those realities, you don't have a music event."

Nonetheless, "music should be free" was the prevailing mentality, and Lang knew exactly how he *didn't* want to see it handled.

"I was in a bunch of festivals that year, and [authorities] were tear-gassing at the gates, people were trying to break in, and there were these sorts of confrontations that were almost preplanned," he said. "I made it sort of, part of the fabric of the festival that there would be free kitchens, free campgrounds, free stages; you could come whether you had money or not. If you wanted to be a part of it, you were in."

In 2009, Lang told *Billboard* that for Woodstock, his solution to crowd control was to provide an experience that festivalgoers themselves would want to keep peaceful.

"We thought from day one that if we did it right, if we gave people more than they were expecting and brought them to nature, everybody would behave and show their best sides,...and that *is* kind of what happened."

Whether Woodstock was a success is a question that the attendees, musicians, and organizers have been grappling with for decades. For Lang, it was less about success versus failure and more about what it symbolized for the long term.

"It was a reaffirming event that made one feel that there was a world out there that could actually survive and become harmonious," he told *Newsday* in 2009.

Four days after Woodstock ended, Lang told *Rolling Stone* that he intended to do another one the next year. He was already thinking about what to do differently.

"Of course, we'll need more room," he said.

It didn't happen, and it would be years before another event bearing the "Woodstock" name would take place. But he never questioned whether Woodstock had been a worthwhile event, and he said so to the *Guardian* in 2012.

"After the three days, I was exhausted and we were in big trouble with the bank, but I still meet people who say it changed their lives," he said. ◆

Promoter Michael Lang gets the news that the stage, which was designed to turn like a lazy Susan, had just stopped functioning. (l-r: Production stage manager Steve Cohen, Lang, Rocky Williams)

Artie Kornfeld

Artie Kornfeld has been a music fan for as long as he can remember. He started off as a child, playing trumpet.

"I was the first tenth-grader that ever made first-chair All-State solo trumpet in the All-State symphony," he said. But when he heard rock and roll for the first time, he fell in love, and he never got over it.

"I wanted to write rock," he said. "I worked a whole summer, simonizing cars, so I could buy a cheap acoustic guitar and get a tape recorder."

He got a record deal, but he saw the most success as a songwriter. He cowrote "Dead Man's Curve," a hit for Jan and Dean, and "The Rain, the Park & Other Things" by the Cowsills, which he also produced.

He moved up the music industry ladder quickly, becoming vice president of Capitol Records when he was still in his twenties. Even then, he identified as a music fan, first and foremost.

"I always felt I was a groupie," he said. "I was just shocked that I was even there with these people. Every time I sat and talked to John Lennon for an hour or two, I couldn't believe I was sitting with John Lennon for two hours."

In 1968, Kornfeld met Michael Lang, who was in New York to promote a band called the Train.

"I got the reputation among producers and musicians and people, you know, 'If you can't get the door open, call Artie Kornfeld'," he said. "I will see you and give you a chance, and I did."

Michael Lang showed up at Capitol without an appointment, and Kornfeld's secretary mentioned that he, like Kornfeld, was from the Brooklyn neighborhood of Bensonhurst. The pair soon became fast friends.

"We immediately hit it off that way, you know," he said. "We didn't hit it off the other way, because I hadn't even done drugs before Woodstock. I hadn't even smoked a joint before Woodstock."

Kornfeld said that he and Lang got an embryonic idea for Woodstock during a long night of hanging out and kicking around ideas.

"It was three in the morning, and I said, 'You know, Michael, it would be great to have a concert at a Broadway theater...I'll just spend all my money, I don't care if I spend it all. And we just keep on getting acts and then make it free and see what happens'."

> *It was three in the morning, and I said, "You know, Michael, it would be great to have a concert at a Broadway theater... I'll just spend all my money, I don't care if I spend it all. And we just keep on getting acts and then make it free and see what happens."*
>
> **—ARTIE KORNFELD**

Kornfeld credited his wife, Linda, with the idea of taking the concept outdoors. But it might not have been successful without his knowledge of the music business, and it also never would have made its money back if he hadn't negotiated with Warner Bros. over the rights to what would become the *Woodstock* documentary.

"I made the movie deal four days before Woodstock," he said.

Kornfeld said that to him, Woodstock wasn't just a musical event. It was a political statement.

"I was very antiwar," he said. "My grandfather's brother was the president of the American Socialist Party, and Woodstock was a very socialist event. Woodstock proved that socialism could work." ◆

Joel Rosenman

Joel Rosenman was one of the two men who gave Woodstock its financial backing, along with John Roberts. According to Artie Kornfeld, there would have been no festival without them.

"It never would have happened without Joel and John putting up that first $270,000," he said.

A musician and a Yale Law School graduate, Rosenman wanted to entertain and wanted to go into business. He split the difference by starting a venture capital company with Roberts, but he had an ulterior motive—they would write a sitcom about two men looking for investment opportunities and find material for it by running a classified ad asking for that very thing.

Kornfeld and Michael Lang responded to the ad, looking for backing for a recording studio. Rosenman and Roberts were already

backing one and weren't interested in another, but they liked the idea of a Bob Dylan concert, which Lang and Kornfeld had proposed as a way of celebrating their new studio, if it opened.

Dylan didn't perform at Woodstock, and Lang and Kornfeld didn't build a recording studio. But the idea of putting on some kind of outdoor concert event had legs, and the four men formed Woodstock Ventures.

"We had to dig deep into our knowledge of what people in general want, what the generation itself wanted, and what we needed to avoid," Rosenman said.

He described the four members of Woodstock Ventures as very different people. But they made it work by finding balance among themselves, as a business entity and as individuals. He said that it was similar to the way that the Woodstock audience functioned.

"The way it came together at the organizational level was an analog of the way the audience came together," he said. "People who didn't know each other kind of bonded in this huge, half-a-million-strong community."

Despite the months of planning and advance preparation, August 15 came and not everything was ready. Woodstock Ventures had to make a decision—either finish building the fences, so no one could get in without a ticket, or finish building the stage, so the bands could perform. They chose the stage and declared Woodstock a free concert, thereby guarantee-

> *We had to dig deep into our knowledge of what people in general want, what the generation itself wanted, and what we needed to avoid.*
>
> **—JOEL ROSENMAN**

ing that they would spend years trying to get out of debt.

"All the decisions that we were making were designed to keep that crowd as happy as possible," he said.

"We told them from the stage, 'the world is watching', 'it's a free concert', 'no one is making a profit from your misery',...and it was to say, 'this could be a big, happy, loving community, where everybody supports everybody else, nobody is taking advantage of anybody.'"

It worked, but it cost them. Rosenman and Roberts lost over a million dollars on Woodstock, and it wasn't until the 1980s that the books were written in black ink, thanks in large part to the box-office take of the *Woodstock* documentary.

Over the years, conventional wisdom has held that Rosenman and Roberts represented the straitlaced, business-oriented faction of Woodstock Ventures, while Kornfeld and Lang were the freewheeling, counterculture faction. This undersells everybody who was involved, including Rosenman, who has always allowed his intuition to guide his decisions.

This was never clearer than in 2009, when he told *The New York Times* that the upcoming fortieth anniversary of Woodstock would have an event associated with it only if it felt right. Despite the high probability that there would have been a lot of money in it,

Promoter Joel Rosenman in 1994, twenty-five years after the Woodstock festival took place, and just a decade after it turned a profit.

all he cared about was whether it passed the smell test.

"If it's not the best lineup and the best setting and the right feeling about the community that develops, we shouldn't have that event," he told the *Times*. ◆

John Roberts

"The day after that festival, we were $2,600,000 in the hole," said Woodstock production coordinator John Morris. "John Roberts and Joel—but it was John's inheritance—were faced after the festival with a tremendous debt and bankers said, 'You have to go bankrupt or pay the money.'"

> *If anyone was not a member of the counterculture, it was John. He dressed like a member of the establishment, he did establishment things. He was the kind that gets rushed to the guillotine when the revolution happens, except that he was adored by everybody, so that no matter what happened, he would have been one of the chosen few.*
>
> **—JOEL ROSENMAN**

Morris said that Roberts, whom he characterized as "a real Edwardian gentleman," wouldn't hear of it.

"John said, 'We are not burdening anybody on this festival; we will pay all the bills'," he said. "And Joel said, 'I agree.'"

Roberts, the fourth member of Woodstock Ventures, was Joel Rosenman's business partner, so it's accurate to say that they took on the financial risk for the festival jointly. But the resources to do that came from Roberts's family, who owned the Block Drug Company, makers of such products as Poli-Grip, Sensodyne, and Beano.

Rosenman and Roberts became close friends after Rosenman's brother arranged a golf game for the three of them. He said that it was surprising that Roberts would back Woodstock, simply because it wasn't his world.

"If anyone was not a member of the counterculture, it was John," Rosenman said. "He dressed like a member of the establishment, he did establishment things. He was the kind that gets rushed to the guillotine when the revolution happens, except that he was adored by everybody, so that no matter what happened, he would have been one of the chosen few."

When Woodstock was done, Morris told *Rolling Stone* that Roberts had taken out $1.3 million in loans to pay off the debts that had been incurred.

"Michael created the energy, John the wherewithal," Morris said. "The energy was a success. The wherewithal was massacred."

Other than an involvement in Woodstock '94, Roberts mostly stayed out of the music business after the original festival. He didn't need it. He had many other interests, which he was happy to pursue.

"By the time I met him, he was already a well-known contract bridge player, duplicate bridge player, and used to play at the highest levels with some of the best players in the world," Rosenman said. "He taught me how to play backgammon, and the two of us used to have an endless amount of fun privately playing, and he would drag me to a tournament in Las Vegas, which seems totally extravagant and stupid. But we won! And we won because he was so imaginative and willing to look at new strategies."

Roberts died in 2001 at the age of fifty-six, from three kinds of cancer—lymphoma, leukemia, and lung cancer.

"He didn't pay much attention to conventional wisdom about health, and if you mentioned his smoking or foods that had too much fat in them, he would say, 'I'm not interested in that kind of a life, I don't want a life where I've ironed out the little imperfections'," Rosenman said. "He'd have some philosophical quotes as to why he was still smoking two packs a day. 'I have no intention of Swiss-ifying my lifestyle.' To be like Switzerland, the symbol of a little country that couldn't take a stand about anything."

Promoter John Roberts in 1994. Joel Rosenman said of Roberts, who passed away in 2001, that he was "adored by everybody."

Although the better part of twenty years has gone by since Roberts's passing, one gets the sense from speaking with Rosenman that he still deeply feels the loss.

"I've been so lucky that I have a big social circle of people that I admire and adore throughout my whole life," he said. "But I would say the closest friend I've ever had in that group was John, and that was from the moment I met him." ◆

John Morris

John Morris was Woodstock's production coordinator and part-time emcee. This has led many people to assume, wrongly, that he was the one who made the announcement warning festivalgoers to stay away from the brown acid. He set the record straight about that.

"[Stage lighting designer Chip Monck] did that announcement," he said. "I get credited with that, and I did not do it. I did not do drugs, because I was usually in charge and I didn't feel I could. So me saying the brown acid is not particularly good would be very out of character, because I would not have the vaguest idea."

Morris worked at the Fillmore East, first helping to set up the venue and then creating shows with such groups as the Grateful Dead and Jefferson Airplane.

"The main thing I was being hired to do was to supervise the production, the stage, and other things, and to help book the artists for the show," he said.

When the time to prepare for Woodstock came, a person's individual specialty was less important than the prevailing sense of "just make it happen." Morris, and the people he worked with, relied on some unorthodox methods as a result.

"We used Boy Scout manuals and US Army field manuals to plan for toilets and stuff," he said. "Of course, we thought we were going to have fifty to seventy-five thousand people, not half a million."

When Morris was deputized to make stage announcements, he said that the job was made easier by the fact that the audience was compliant.

"We asked them to take care of each other; we asked them to cooperate," he said. "I mean, during the storm, I was asking people to get off the towers, because the towers were dangerous, and they got off the towers."

The crowd was even responsive when informed that an anarchist group from New York City called the Crazies planned to descend on the festival and destroy the concession stands. This was capitalism, the Crazies reasoned, and it needed to be smashed.

"When they came running out of the woods, they got smothered by about fifty thousand people who said, 'Nah man, you don't want to do that', and saved the concession stands," he said.

"One of the major things about Woodstock, and to me it's the greatest example, is that Woodstock got a lot of people to do stuff they wouldn't have normally done, and help other people totally selflessly," Morris added. "I mean, [there were] just a tremendous amount of people who did that."

After the festival, Morris said that he and Woodstock artist coordinator Bill Belmont were asked to work on the Altamont Festival in California. They refused, a decision that looks good in retrospect.

"They were going to cut corners and they were going to make mistakes, and the place was a ghastly site," he said. Despite the violence and chaos that happened there, he said that subsequent festivals repeated many of the same mistakes.

"In other places down the line, they tried to just multiply the number of people that were at Woodstock, times whatever kiddie prize they had, and thought they were going to become multibillionaires," he said. "It didn't work that way."

Today, Morris produces art and antique shows in Santa Fe and San Francisco. But despite the fact that Woodstock is firmly in his past, he said that he's proud to this day that he helped make an unforgettable weekend for over 400,000 people. He also said that there could have been even more.

Woodstock production coordinator John Morris, who received repeated electrical shocks when he made announcements from the stage in the rain.

"They showed me satellite photographs," he said. "It showed that two million people more were trying to get into that field."

Morris said that the organizers' knowledge of the music business and the flexibility of the people working it were what made the festival a success.

"What you had was a group of young people who had been in the music business, and who understood the music business, which was really just on its first legs, doing things that forced them to think outside of the box," he said. ◆

People, given a chance, will rise to the occasion. And in this case, you had a tremendous number of people who rose to the occasion. The Indians up in that area, the Hog Farmers, people just with other people, who shared in and worked their way through it.

—JOHN MORRIS

Chris Langhart

Chris Langhart was Woodstock's technical director. John Morris called him "an absolute, flat-out genius...the person who could anticipate and think of what we might miss."

If we had more time, it would have been more organized.

—CHRIS LANGHART

Morris recalled one event just prior to the festival that impressed him greatly.

"Langhart came in and said, 'How much does Jimi Hendrix weigh?'"

Morris guessed 160 pounds. Langhart returned to his trailer, returning later to ask what the average groupie weighed. Morris guessed 125 pounds. Langhart disappeared again and returned hours later with the design for the bridge to the festival stage.

"He had loaded it, taking Hendrix's weight and as many groupies as you could possibly get on the bridge chasing him," Morris said. "He tripled that and made that the loading quotient for the bridge. The bridge was excellent, and it took two decent bulldozers about a day and a half to pull it down after the festival."

Langhart and his crew of approximately 130 people outfitted the grounds with electricity and running water. They spread out across the field, relying on decades-old communication methods to relay information.

"We had [hand-cranked field phones], those World War I, World War II kind of things, where you run a wire in the trench," Langhart said. "You had to crank on the telephone and it would ring and you would get a hold of somebody."

Outfitting the field with running water was successful, even if it would never hold up as a permanent water system.

"You knew where you wanted to run the line, and where the well was, and where the spigots were," he said. "You just put the thing on the ground wherever it needed to be."

Langhart said that the two-and-a-half weeks that were available to get everything up and running forced him and his crew to find engineering solutions that he wasn't crazy about.

"If we had more time, it would have been more organized," he said. "But I don't think anybody figured on building a water system in the field, laid out in a sort of orderly engineering fashion."

A bridge (and its permit application) designed by technical director Chris Langhart to withstand the weight of Jimi Hendrix and as many groupies as might be chasing him.

Equipping the site with running water may not have turned out exactly the way he wanted, but it worked. Getting the stage built as designed, on the other hand, simply wasn't possible.

"The roof wouldn't support itself, so it never got any lights put on it," he said. As a result, all the lighting was provided by follow spots.

Langhart also didn't like where the heliport was. Woodstock Ventures had hired helicopters to bring the performers to and from the site, and they landed so close to the performers' pavilion that postconcert interviews were impossible, due to the noise.

"There would have been many wonderful interviews with artists had the artists' space been further from the heliport," he said. However, he conceded that it was the only option. "The heliport was put in the only place it could be put by the time things got going."

Langhart said that his experience with Woodstock didn't end when the festival did. He had been instrumental in making a field inhabitable for over 400,000 hippies, so the government branded him a dangerous subversive and tapped his phone for a year.

"Looking back on it, you can see that this is the second-largest city in the state of New York, which happened in two and a half weeks," he said. "If you were the Civil Defense Authority, you would want to know why that was." ◆

Chip Monck

Woodstock lighting designer Chip Monck (left) with Joshua White (right) of the Joshua Light Show.

When it comes to stage lighting design, John Morris was unqualified in his praise for Chip Monck, the man who he said was the best in the business.

"Chip is the best rock-and-roll lighting designer ever," he said.

As if to underscore the point, Monck won the Parnelli Lifetime Achievement Award in 2004, the staging and lighting industry's highest honor.

Before Woodstock, Monck was already well known in the music and theater world. He had worked at the Newport Folk Festival, the Newport Jazz Festival, and the Apollo Theater.

He heard about Woodstock through Hector Morales of the William Morris Agency, whom he would contact every couple of weeks to find new work.

"I went to Hector, and he said, 'Oh, by the way, this guy Michael Lang, here's his number, he's hiring everything in Christendom, I suggest you get in touch with him.' Michael and I started to chat about what I could do, what I do, what I did, and how could I help."

There were only a couple of weeks to get the Bethel site into shape, and one of the casualties of the time crunch was the stage, which had been designed by stage production manager Steve Cohen.

"What we should have had was five Navajo riggers who were the best in the oil business, and maybe four or five Texas, heavy-duty, redneck oil workers that could have put the staging together as it should have been, but we didn't," he said. "We had one person that was on the crane, standing in a fifty-five-gallon drum, trying to tighten nuts and bolts to keep things in the air."

Monck also served as Woodstock's other emcee, along with John Morris. He said that he was drafted into the role by Michael Lang, who had forgotten to hire one in all the chaos. His first announcement was a request for everyone close to the stage to please take ten large steps back.

Monck maintained a cordial but assertive tone in his announcements. He believed them to be just as effective as those that he had seen that same year in Boston with the Rolling Stones.

"In Boston Garden, it was 'Shut the fuck up, this is your mayor, Kevin White, he has a few things to say to you, so listen'," he said.

Monck made announcements from the stage on behalf of the concertgoers, much of them conveyed to him on any surface that happened to be handy and could make its way onstage.

"One of them was a sneaker with a little note about, 'Please have Joe meet me with my diabetic pills at so and so', which of course had nothing to do with diabetes," he said. "It had to do with his grass. But you read it anyway, and then you put it aside."

After Woodstock, Monck went on to work other rock festivals, including the violence-plagued Altamont festival. Despite the way that that turned out, he kept working for the Rolling Stones for the next five years. Today, he lives in Australia, where he works in corporate and retail lighting, and where he's much less likely to have his teeth knocked out by speed-addled bikers with pool cues. ◆

The scaffolding was up, but the stage was still in progress, which meant that lighting designer Chip Monck's 650,000 watts' worth of equipment spent the weekend under the stage.

Bill Hanley

Bill Hanley is known as "the Father of Festival Sound." Woodstock was one of his most high-profile jobs.

"I was trying to find someone who could do a sound system for Woodstock, and there was no one who had ever done something like that before," Michael Lang told *Front of House Online*. "Then there was this crazy guy in Boston who might want to take a shot at it."

Hanley said that he became interested in audio at a very young age, thanks to his local roller rink. He was enchanted by the sound quality of its organ, which was leaps and bounds ahead of anything he had ever heard.

"I would go hear other, bad sound systems and wonder why something couldn't sound as good as that roller rink," he told *Front of House Online*.

He took it upon himself to locate venues where the sound system was less than ideal and bring them up to speed.

"I ended up going down to Newport, where they had audio problems," he said. "I was running the sound system because the guy that bought some good equipment up there really wasn't interested in making events happen well, audiowise."

Eventually, word got out. Hanley did sound for the Beach Boys, and then for the Beatles in 1966.

> *I was doing a whole lot of groups around the country when they were going on tour. I was with Jefferson Airplane, went to Europe with them, you name it. I was really the first guy to do it and chase after the acts to try to improve things.*
>
> **—BILL HANLEY**

"I was doing a whole lot of groups around the country when they were going on tour," he said. "I was with Jefferson Airplane, went to Europe with them, you name it. I was really the first guy to do it and chase after the acts to try to improve things."

He got a call from Michael Lang, who offered Hanley the Woodstock job based on what he had done over the past few years. Hanley said that he had lofty goals for the sound quality that he wanted to provide.

"I wanted to have a sound like the sound that you do in the recording studio, without multitracking," he said.

Hanley said that despite the fact that he was doing sound for the entire festival, he wasn't able to listen to the music and enjoy it in the way that the audience did.

"No, I was working," he said. "I was trying to figure how to kill this parasitic oscillation problem."

Regardless, Hanley's work won raves from the people he worked with.

"I thought the sound was great, and everyone I talked to thought the sound was great," Lang told *Front of House Online*. "Everyone could hear, nothing blew up, and it all hung together perfectly."

Lighting designer and part-time Woodstock emcee Chip Monck also weighed in, describing Hanley as "a great concept person, a visionary. He never had a negative word to say, only wanting a stable power supply and a bit more time."

Hanley ran into professional problems after the festival. Rather than giving his career a

"I thought the sound was great, and everyone I talked to thought the sound was great," promoter Michael Lang said of the work performed by sound engineer Bill Hanley (above).

higher profile, the Woodstock gig made authorities decide to crack down on the menace of music festivals across the board.

"I ended up losing $400,000 worth of work because the government attacked the whole festival scene," he said. "They put together the Mass Gathering Act, and then all the festivals had to cancel."

Hanley stopped chasing big festival jobs and shifted his focus to venues where he could work without worry. Today, he works on dance and classical music performances.

"They thank me for my work because now you could write music for the violins and they could be heard for a change," he said.

Like Chip Monck, in 2006 Hanley received the Parnelli Lifetime Achievement Award. ◆

The Hog Farm

One of the best decisions that the Woodstock promoters made was to fly in a hundred members of the Hog Farm commune from New Mexico. The group was led by Hugh Romney, better known as Wavy Gravy.

They were described as working security for the festival, but that doesn't really capture what they did.

Ethel Romm of the *Times Herald-Record*, one of the few publications that covered Woodstock from the scene, wrote in the *Huffington Post* in 2009 that one of the things the collective did was tend to people having bad drug experiences, such as a young woman who appeared on the paper's front page, being carried on a stretcher to the First Aid tent.

"The Hog Farm was probably there within ten minutes, comforting her, which would have made a truer picture [than the stretcher] of how bad drug reactions were handled," she said.

> *Thanks to Hog Farm, I didn't starve.*
> —DIKKO FAUST

The Hog Farm accepted the help of anyone who wanted to pitch in. This included seventeen-year-old Dikko Faust, an attendee who said that he helped with food prep and whatever else needed to be done.

"I am convinced they saved the festival," he said. "Thanks to Hog Farm, I didn't starve."

Wavy Gravy said that the Hog Farm was approached by Michael Lang about working Woodstock while they were in New York City. At the time, the collective was based in New Mexico, and when Lang offered to fly them out, he assumed that Lang, whom he described as "looking like Allen Ginsberg on a Dick Gregory diet," was just talking drug-addled nonsense, so he disregarded it.

"However, there we were, Summer Solstice on a Tesuque Indian reservation, and this guy shows up with one of those slightly aluminum rock-and-roll briefcases, and inside there

The Hog Farm area on the festival grounds, where attendees were treated for acid trips gone awry.

is paperwork that indeed we have our own American Airlines AstroJet to take us to Kennedy Airport, eighty-five of us and fifteen Native Americans," he said.

Wavy Gravy said that they were paid "about $600,000 for clearing land," but accepted no money for working security.

"We refused to be paid for being security, because then the various factions would say, 'Oh we're in the pocket of the producers and promoters', whereas if we didn't take money, we were an independent entity," he said.

The Hog Farm also ran the Freak-Out Tent, a refuge for festivalgoers who had taken LSD to bad effect.

"This guy comes in, he's like, 'Miami Beach...Joyce...Joyce...1944'," Wavy Gravy said. "I leaned in and I said, 'What's your name, man?' He says, 'Joyce...Miami Beach.' I said to him, 'Your name.'"

The man revealed that his name was Bob, and Wavy Gravy said, "Your name is Bob" back to him. After Gravy repeated Bob's name a couple of times, Bob began to calm down.

"You took a little acid," Wavy Gravy said to him. "It's going to wear off."

When it wore off, the Hog Farm deputized Bob to calm down new people that came into the tent with bad acid experiences, just as they had brought Bob back down to earth a little while earlier.

"'You see that sister coming through the door with her toes in her nose? That was you four hours ago, now you're the doctor, take over,'" he told Bob, and then the person that Bob helped would pick up the next shift. "As one person was cured, he became the doctor to help out the next person," Wavy Gravy said. ◆

The Hog Farm collective set up shop on the festival grounds to serve brown rice, talk people down from bad trips, and keep everyone fed and happy.

Bill Graham

Concert promoter Bill Graham had no formal involvement with Woodstock, but it's hard to imagine it happening without him. He was the first to present the music of the counterculture as a marketable commodity, and without that, August 15 would have been just another sleepy Friday in the Catskills.

After serving in the Korean War, he settled in San Francisco and met the San Francisco Mime Troupe, a political satire organization that regularly ran afoul of the law. When members of the troupe were arrested on obscenity charges, Graham organized a benefit concert for them, featuring the Fugs and Jefferson Airplane.

He quickly established credibility with the city's psychedelic underground, and he recognized its commercial potential. This inspired him to host "Bill Graham Presents" shows at the Fillmore Auditorium, which helped start the careers of such future Woodstock acts as Janis Joplin and Jimi Hendrix.

He came to New York in 1968 to open the Fillmore East. This venue would employ such talents as Chris Langhart, Chip Monck, and Joshua White, all of whom would work at Woodstock.

Graham had offered guidance to the Monterey Pop Festival organizers, and he did the same for Woodstock Ventures. Sometimes, they took his advice, sometimes they didn't.

"When I went to see Bill, he said, 'Look, it's simple. You dig a trench around the stage, because you've got to protect the stage'," Joel Rosenman said. "'And you fill the trench with oil, and then if they try to rush to the stage, you light the oil... I think dogs would be helpful, the guards should have dogs.'"

Woodstock Ventures did not take this advice.

In 2009, Michael Lang said that he had asked Graham to emcee the Woodstock festival.

"He declined with a typical Bill comment," Lang told *Billboard*. "'We can't both be God on the same day.'"

Graham also gave Lang a tape of a new band from San Francisco that he was managing. It was Santana, and he wanted them to perform at Woodstock.

"It took me three seconds to say, 'Yes, we'll take them', and it was the best buy I ever made," Lang said.

When Woodstock was over, Graham gave it a mixed review.

> *I had asked Graham to emcee...He declined with a typical Bill comment. "We can't both be God on the same day."*
>
> **—MICHAEL LANG**

Concert promoter Bill Graham in his office at the Fillmore East, the venue where many of the people who worked the Woodstock festival got their start or honed their craft.

"There were thousands of people that were very disappointed, who never got near the site and had to camp out in the middle of nowhere," he said, according to the *San Diego Union Tribune*. Still, he acknowledged that the event was unprecedented.

"Woodstock was the first and there was an attempt to do it right," he acknowledged. "There were a lot of mistakes, but there were no blueprints."

Graham remained a vital force throughout the 1970s and 1980s. His view of the music industry, and of Woodstock, took on a some-

what vinegary overtone, such as when he spoke to the *Los Angeles Times* in 1989 about Janis Joplin, who famously brought a bottle of Southern Comfort on stage when she performed.

"Do you realize that if Woodstock took place now, Southern Comfort would pay her a million dollars for just holding that bottle?" he asked. The question may have stung, but no one could say that he was wrong.

In 1990, Graham was killed in a helicopter crash, along with pilot Steve Kahn and Bill Graham Presents staffer Melissa Gold. He was sixty years old. ◆

Abbie Hoffman

Abbie Hoffman was a political activist who cofounded the Youth International Party, better known as the Yippies. Many people are unaware that he was at Woodstock, and many of those who are only know about an incident that occurred during the Who's set.

"The Who were about to go on, and [Hoffman] told me that there was somebody running around with a gun," Michael Lang said. "Abbie, on his way to the stage, took a few tabs of acid, and once we determined that there wasn't anybody running around with a knife or a gun, I told him to come up on stage to watch the Who, which we did."

If Lang's intent was to get Hoffman to calm down and enjoy the music, it didn't work.

"He wanted to say something about [political activist] John Sinclair being busted for two joints and given fifteen years," Lang said. "He couldn't help himself. Pete [Townshend] turned just as it happened, and Abbie got up and grabbed his mic and started talking about John Sinclair. Pete turned around and saw someone at the mic and swatted him across the back of the head with his guitar. Abbie went down and then off into the crowd."

Jonathan Paley, an audience member who was fourteen, had a different recollection.

"It was a push," he said. "Pete rushed him with his guitar and hit him in the back with his body and his guitar. Abbie went flying down with his hands up in the air, like spread-eagled. It almost looked rehearsed, in a way.

But it was so perfect. He couldn't have done it any better. It was like he was a stuntman going off the stage in full spread-eagled mode."

Townshend had his own recollection.

"I knocked Abbie aside using the headstock of my guitar," he wrote in his memoir, *Who I Am*. "A sharp end of one of my strings must have pierced his skin because he reacted as though stung, retreating to sit cross-legged at the side of the stage."

Hoffman's few seconds onstage have had the unfortunate effect of overshadowing his contributions to Woodstock. He was a valued presence who was instrumental in helping things run smoothly.

"You know who organized the whole scene of creating the hospital?" Wavy Gravy asked. "Sorting out all that stuff that was flown in by a helicopter and what have you? It was Abbie Hoffman, who was a brilliant organizer, and he did it flawlessly and magnificently, and he deserves major kudos for pulling that off."

Lang agreed with Wavy Gravy's account.

"Abbie sort of took over the hospital situation, in terms of supply and organizing supplies, and worked, you know, right up until he came to me backstage," Lang said.

John Morris was also eager to set the record straight.

"Abbie went right to work in the medical tents the minute the festival started and worked as a medical aide throughout the whole thing, until the time when the Who played," he said.

> *You know who organized the whole scene of creating the hospital? Sorting out all that stuff that was flown in by a helicopter and what have you? It was Abbie Hoffman, who was a brilliant organizer, and he did it flawlessly and magnificently, and he deserves major kudos for pulling that off.*
>
> —WAVY GRAVY

Hoffman died in 1989, at the age of fifty-two, in what *The New York Times* said was an apparent suicide. Morris said that it was important to remember his many important contributions that weekend, rather than let them be obscured by a single moment.

"I had known Abbie from running the Fillmore East in New York and we got along pretty well," he said. "Abbie was a real contributor to Woodstock in a lot of ways. He had spent two-and-a-half days before [the Who incident] helping out in the medical tent. He knew that we needed help, and so he helped where he could. There were a lot of people like that, but Abbie doesn't get credit for it. I'll swear on a Bible to the last of my days that that's what Abbie did. I was always grateful to him." ◆

Arnold Skolnick

The original Woodstock poster has a couple of inaccuracies. It cites White Lake, New York, as the venue, and it says that one of the performers on Sunday, August 17, was the Jeff Beck Group.

That's nitpicking, though. The poster, which depicts a catbird perched on the neck of an acoustic guitar, is one of the best known ever to be associated with a musical event.

It was designed by Arnold Skolnick, a commercial artist from Brooklyn. When he was asked to design it, he approached it the same way he approached anything else.

"It was just another job, but it became famous," he told the *Stamford Advocate* in 2010. "It said peace, it said music. It was very colorful, so people did not forget it."

Skolnick wasn't the first artist that Woodstock Ventures approached. David Byrd designed an incredibly intricate poster that was based on the work of nineteenth-century French artist Jean Auguste Dominique Ingres, but it wasn't used.

On his official website, Byrd explained that he delivered his poster as promised, then left town for thirty days. He wasn't around, or reachable, when the venue was moved.

"As I was not available to do a new poster, it was done by another artist, and appropriately became very famous," he said.

There is a difference of opinion as to who came up with the design that was finally used. In Michael Lang's 2009 book, *The Road to Woodstock*, the promoter said that the design was his.

"I gave Arnold the copy and told him the main message was 'three days of peace and music' and that I wanted a dove perched on a guitar as our image," Lang wrote. Skolnick, on the other hand, said that the design was

> *It was just another job, but it became famous. It said peace, it said music. It was very colorful, so people did not forget it.*
>
> **—ARNOLD SKOLNICK**

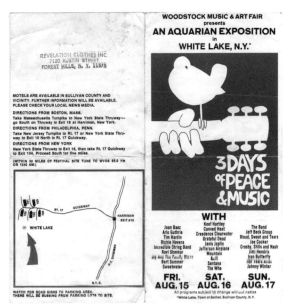

his, and that the line, "three days of peace and music," was the creation of writer Ira Arnold.

Artie Kornfeld, John Morris, and Joel Rosenman all backed Skolnick's version of events, according to *Newsday*.

Skolnick went to Woodstock, but he was so put off by the crowd's size that he and his wife left after the first day. They had to stay at a nearby hotel until traffic subsided enough for them get back to New York City.

"If I had been sixteen or seventeen, I probably would have enjoyed it," he told the *Stamford Advocate*. At the time, though, he was in his early thirties and just not up for it.

After finishing the poster job, Skolnick went right back to work, and eventually founded his own award-winning print com-

pany. But while he may not have gotten much out of the one day he spent at Woodstock, he knows perfectly well that it was a significant event and that it struck a chord with enough people to populate a major city.

"Something was tapped, a nerve, in this country," he said in the book, *Woodstock: Peace, Music & Memories*. "And everybody just came." ◆

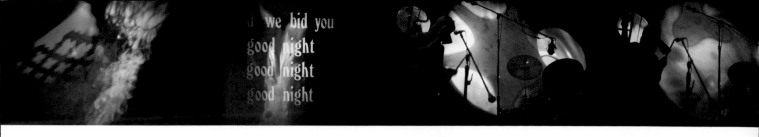

Joshua White

Joshua White is the man behind the Joshua Light Show, a psychedelic, liquid light show that served as a backdrop to many of the bands that played at the Fillmore East.

The light show was hired to work at Woodstock, but very little went as intended.

One of the people who worked with the light show was P. J. Soles, who operated the spotlight and later went on to act in such films as *Carrie*, *Halloween*, and *Rock 'n' Roll High*

The Joshua Light Show, summer 1969. Top row l to r: Thomas Shoesmith, Jane Rixmann, Jon Davison, Gene Thiel, Bill Schwarzbach, Karen Liebman. Bottom row l to r: Stu Hutter, Amalie Rothschild, Ken Richman, Josh White, Cecily Hoyt.

School. At the time, she was nineteen. She said she had never been a part of the counter-culture and had no idea what Woodstock was until White said the company had a job there.

"I have never been a person that would have gone to Woodstock if I hadn't gone with Joshua," she said.

The light show arrived on the Wednesday before Woodstock, and White had already surveyed the site in advance. He had requested what he would need to have the show there, but the time constraints caused by moving from Wallkill to Bethel had compromised many of the things that he had requested.

"They sort of got everything half-done, at the most," Joshua White said. "We ended up having to build our own platform and build a shelter over it, improvise some kind of a trailer, so we could have a place that we could not be on stage."

On Friday, the weather already wasn't cooperating, and that was even before the rain started.

"Winds came up at sunset, so the screen began to blow in the wind," he said. "It become a giant sail, so they began to slash the bottom of it, which made sense—I can't

actually think of any other solution—and we managed to perform through the first night."

Certain things got done, but they didn't have the effect White had intended. At the Fillmore East, the light show used a forty-foot screen. At Woodstock, they had an eighty-foot screen, larger than a standard IMAX screen and a significant upgrade. Even so, it wasn't big enough, which White realized the instant that he saw the finished product.

"At the Fillmore, you looked at the stage and there was this giant screen, and you saw the musicians and you saw the light show," he said. "It made everything big. At Woodstock, it made nothing big. It was just there. And that was really the most depressing part of all."

The Joshua Light Show left Woodstock the next day. They had planned to work the entire weekend, but when they returned to the site on Saturday, the eighty-foot screen was missing.

"I said, 'What happened?' and they said, 'Oh, the screen blew away'," he recalled. "Well, no screen, no light show. So, we took our stuff, packed it on the truck, and left."

White learned the true fate of the screen while watching the *Woodstock* documentary in 1970.

"You could see the stage crew ripping up the screen to use as tarpaulins, because it hadn't occurred to them to get any kind of rain

covers for the instruments or everything," he said. "The screen became the world's most expensive drop cloth."

In 1970, White left the company that he had founded to create Joshua Television, which was similar to the light show but was generated electronically and shown on video screens. This allowed him to make the jump from small venues to places like Madison Square Garden.

White returned to the light show in the new millennium, and it still exists today. He said fifty years after the fact that even if the experience wasn't quite what he intended, he was happy to be a part of the Woodstock story. ◆

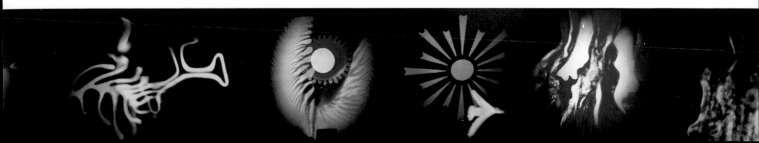

YASGUR

Yasgur Rd

THE LAST PIECE OF
YASGUR FARM STILL
HELD BY THE FAMILY
MRS. YASGUR SOLD ALL BUT 1 SQ. FT.
OF THE FARM, THIS LAST PIECE
WILL ALWAYS REMAIN IN HER FAMILY
AFFECTIONATELY DEDICATED BY ROY & JERYL'S FAMILY

SOUTH
New York

Yasgur Farms
DAIRY

Max Yasgur

Max Yasgur was a dairy farmer in Bethel, New York. He allowed the promoters to use his land when the original site in Wallkill fell through. It was not because he shared the promoters' beliefs.

"He was older, he was Republican, he was pro the war, but he was the most fair-minded person I've ever known," Michael Lang said. "He just wanted to give us the opportunity that he felt we deserved."

Woodstock was originally supposed to take place in the town of Woodstock, New York. When that fell through, Lang said that Joel Rosenman and John Roberts found an industrial park in Wallkill. That fell through as well.

"The town decided that they were being invaded by all these hippies and passed a law, the terms of which we couldn't meet," Lang said. The law had been hastily invented, specifically to stop the promoters from holding the festival there.

"I think it was 'Local Law Number One,'" Lang said.

Miraculously, the eventual site was found the very next day. Lang was on his way to look at a different site, and on the drive there, he saw Yasgur's field and thought it was perfect. Lang had a meeting with him that could best be described as a "cold call," and a deal was made.

Woodstock Ventures may have been up against the clock, but in truth, both parties needed each other.

"It was a bad summer for [Yasgur's] hay crop," Lang said. "He had the biggest dairy farm in the area and he needed to buy hay, so he needed some money."

Lang said that they agreed to rent the property for $50,000.

Many residents of Sullivan County were livid. According to the book, *Woodstock Revisited: 50 Far Out, Groovy, Peace-Loving, Flashback-Inducing Stories from Those Who Were There*, Yasgur found signs bordering on

Max Yasgur flashes the peace sign after addressing "the largest group of people ever assembled in one place."

his property urging people not to buy his milk because "he loves hippies."

"The sign did it," Yasgur's wife, Miriam, said in *Haaretz*. "When Max saw that, I knew darned well he was going to let them have their festival."

Yasgur attended a town board meeting to address the attempts to stop the festival. He asked if the gathering violated any existing laws. It didn't.

"So the only objection to having a festival here is to keep longhairs out of town?" he asked, according to *Woodstock Revisited*. "Well, you can all go pound salt up your ass, because come August 15, we're going to have a festival!"

On Sunday, August 17, just before Joe Cocker performed, the dairy farmer came onstage. If the preceding days of electric guitars, nudity, and LSD had worn thin for him, it didn't show when he stepped up to the microphone.

"This is the largest group of people ever assembled in one place, and I think you have proven something to the world, that a half a million kids can get together for three days of fun and music and nothing but fun and music, and I bless you for it," he said.

Yasgur suffered a fatal heart attack in 1973. He's still remembered with great affection today, both by the people who knew him personally and by those who just knew who he was and what he did. ◆

THERE ARE IMAGES THAT WILL NEVER LEAVE MY MIND. IT COULD BE COMPARED TO PTSD, EXCEPT THEY'RE PLEASANT.

—Jim Mesthene

I FOUND IT ALL TO BE VERY TRAUMATIZING. I'M STILL NOT THE OUTDOORS TYPE, SO OUT IN THE RAIN I FOUND IT VERY UPSETTING. IF ANYONE SAYS THEY HAD A GOOD TIME THERE, THEY ARE EITHER LYING OR THEY WERE ON DRUGS.

—JoAnn Devitt

I DON'T THINK ANYONE THERE HAD A CAMERA. MAYBE SOME PEOPLE DID, BUT IT'S NOT LIKE YOU HAD A CELL PHONE IN YOUR POCKET.

—Marla Argintar

Word of Mouth

In today's era of flash mobs organized in minutes on Twitter, it's hard to fathom how the word got out so effectively about Woodstock. But the number of people who showed up speaks volumes about how effective simple word of mouth was.

"That was accomplished because a hundred thousand kids each told four other kids," Joel Rosenman said. "That was one kid talking to another kid on the phone, or at baseball practice."

Dan Sorenson, who was twenty, heard about it at a local record shop in Rockville, Maryland.

"In the pre-Internet days, there was a whole different deal trying to know where live music performances were going to be," he said. "I remember buying my tickets at the record store, probably a few weeks in advance."

Roberta Becker, who was seventeen, was at a clothing store in Forest Hills, Queens, New York.

"My friend and I walked into Revelation," Becker said. "They had posters up, and it looked like fun. There was no Ticketron then; you bought the tickets from the guy at the cash register."

Vince Scarlata, who was also twenty, heard about Woodstock at a head shop in New York City.

"I used to hang out in the West Village, and walking down MacDougal Street, all the head shops had the advertisements in the window."

Posters and underground publications served the function that event reminders on Facebook serve today. The difference is that those methods actually worked.

"Our media buys, which were all underground media, were probably the newspaper analog of the head shop," Rosenman said. "The *East Village Other* and the *Rat*, and the *Village Voice*."

JoAnn Devitt, who was sixteen and hailed from Boston, said that she didn't remember hearing about Woodstock in a specific place. She just remembered a persistent buzz about it that never really died down until it was over.

"It was just generally advertised," she said. "I hung around a lot of people who were in bands, and everybody wanted to go."

If you were the type of person who hung out with musicians and went to see live music on a regular basis, Woodstock was easy to hear about. Marla Argintar, who was nineteen, lived in a big house in Burlington, Vermont, that often served as a crash pad for touring musicians.

"Edgar Winter came to town, or it was Johnny, his brother, and they ended up staying in our house for a month," she said. "I lived with a couple of people that were musicians… people that were into music. I guess we heard there was going to be a concert, so we said, 'Let's go.'"

There was also that old standby for spreading music news—the radio. Jim Mesthene, who was sixteen, said that he heard about Woodstock on WBZ AM, a Boston Top 40 radio station.

"They just listed the bands who were going to be there, and I said, 'Well yeah, I'm going'," he said. ◆

Artists Who Didn't Perform

Some of the biggest names in music turned down invitations to play at Woodstock. Others accepted the offer but then canceled, and others accepted but simply couldn't get there.

THE JEFF BECK GROUP

The Jeff Beck Group was scheduled to appear on Sunday, but before the event, the guitarist canceled the appearance and broke up the band.

"I deliberately broke the group up before Woodstock," Beck said, according to the book *How the Fender Bass Changed the World*, by Annette Carson and Jay Roberts. "I didn't want it to be preserved. Even though we were playing really well, the vibes in the band were totally shredded."

THE DOORS

Michael Lang said that he wanted to book the Doors, but singer Jim Morrison didn't want to perform.

"I think the things that happened to him at Miami had him really screwed up," John Morris said, referring to the singer's March 1969 arrest for indecent exposure, which had a profound effect on his emotional state.

"Jim was a little paranoid that he was going to get shot on stage," Lang said.

BOB DYLAN

"[Bob Dylan] was very reluctant to be in the middle of an event like that, because he had been sort of the savior of the sixties in a lot of people's minds, and they were invading his privacy," Michael Lang said.

"It seemed like this was just much more of a burden for him than it needed to be," he said. He invited Dylan to perform anyway, but the singer said no.

IRON BUTTERFLY

Iron Butterfly was on the way to perform at Woodstock when they were stranded at New York City's LaGuardia Airport. They demanded that the promoters come fetch them by helicopter, in a way that was not to John Morris's liking.

"Iron Butterfly sent me a telegram saying, 'We're at LaGuardia Airport, you will send a helicopter down to pick us up, you will fly us to the site, we will immediately play, and then we will get in the same helicopter and fly back to wherever it was, LaGuardia or whatever'," Morris said.

He sent a telegram back to tell them that the services of both the group and its seventeen-minute drum solos were no longer required, in an acrostic that read as follows:

For reasons I can't go into
Until you are here
Clarifying your situation
Knowing you are having problems

You will have to find
Other transportation
Unless you plan not to come

LED ZEPPELIN

Led Zeppelin was a new band when they were invited to perform at Woodstock, but they already had rock-star attitude down pat. They refused to perform because they didn't want to share a stage with anyone else. "That's what the feedback was that we got, although they played at other festivals that summer," Michael Lang said.

JOHN LENNON

John Lennon was invited to perform, but Lang said that the soon-to-be-former Beatle was unable to enter the United States.

"I did want to get John Lennon in to perform, but he couldn't get into the country," Lang said.

JONI MITCHELL

Mitchell was invited to perform at Woodstock but turned it down on the advice of her manager, who wanted her to stay in Manhattan ahead of her scheduled appearance on *The Dick Cavett Show*, according to the *New York Daily News*.

Not being there didn't stop her from writing the song "Woodstock," which was a hit for Crosby, Stills, Nash & Young, and which has led many people to assume, wrongly, that she performed there.

THE MOODY BLUES

"One of the groups that I was really looking forward to hearing was the Moody Blues," said Don Stark, an audience member who was seventeen. The group was scheduled to perform but had to scrap their plans.

"They were booked, but they were unable to come because they weren't finished with their album, and they decided to stay in the studio," Lang said.

ROY ROGERS

Jimi Hendrix famously closed Woodstock, but if Lang had had his way, it would have ended quite differently.

"The other one who turned me down was Roy Rogers," he said. "I wanted to close with him singing, 'Happy Trails.'" ◆

The Locals

Bethel is a sleepy, rural town of roughly four thousand people, consisting mostly of farmland and resorts. The people who descended on it over the weekend of August 15, 1969, were sometimes at odds with the people who lived there, but by most accounts, they got along.

This was because the kids failed to live up to the locals' worst nightmares, and the locals refused to let the kids go hungry.

"Notwithstanding their personality, their dress, and their ideas, they were and they are the most courteous, considerate, and well-behaved group of kids I have ever been in contact with in my twenty-four years of police work," said Lou Yank, chief of police in the nearby town of Monticello, in *The New York Times*.

Rolling Stone reported that the local telephone switchboard, which fielded 500,000 long-distance calls on Friday alone, shared the sentiment. A local operator said that "every kid said thank you."

Local police had similar attitudes to report. "When our police cars were getting stuck, they even helped us get them out," a local police officer told *Rolling Stone*. "It was really amazing."

Not everyone had the same experience, though. According to *Rolling Stone*, local vegetable farmer Herman Reinshagen said that some of the attendees rifled through his crops, helping themselves to beets, carrots, corn, and whatever else happened to be within reach.

Local resident Ben Leon, meanwhile, was so enraged at being kept up by the revelry that he went full "Okie from Muskogee" in an effort to shut them up.

Thursday, August 14, 1969.
In 24 hours, Bethel, New York,
would never again be an unknown,
sleepy town in the Catskills.

"They were making so much noise I had to come out with my .30-06 and I shot it ten times into the air," Leon said. "That got them moving."

The occasional gunplay notwithstanding, the citizens of Sullivan County stepped up to ease the food situation. When reports of shortages made the news, locals made thousands of donations of canned goods, fruit, sandwiches, and water.

The Women's Group of the Jewish Community Center in Monticello donated thirty thousand sandwiches that they had prepared. These were distributed by the Sisters of the Convent of St. Thomas.

The armed forces chipped in, too. On the morning of August 17, Air Force helicopters brought in three hundred pounds of food. Sheriff Lou Radner of Sullivan County said that his county flew in an Army helicopter with food, blankets, and medical supplies, in an air drop that included water, fruit, canned goods, and sandwiches, according to the *Huffington Post*.

"From the back, I could see standing on the stage a couple of Hueys flying in our direction, and I could also see red crosses on the side of the helicopters," said John Morris. "I said, 'Ladies and gentlemen would you please welcome the United States Army', and there was a boo. And I said 'Medical Corps' and it changed into a gigantic cheer."

Local residents had many reasons to help out, from sincere compassion to simply not wanting their area to become synonymous with disaster. Whatever the reason, the locals should be recognized for what they did, when the easiest thing in the world would have been to turn their backs on the kids who had come to their area. ◆

SO A LOT OF PEOPLE CAME WITH SLEEPING BAGS AND PLANNING ON SLEEPING OUT. WHAT THEY DIDN'T PLAN ON WAS THAT THE GROUND WOULD BE A SEA OF MUD. SO, THAT WAS LOGISTICALLY PROBLEMATIC. THEN AGAIN, PEOPLE WERE SO STONED, THEY DIDN'T CARE.

—Carol Clapp

Getting There

Marla Argintar was nineteen when she went to Woodstock. She had no idea what the scale of the event was going to be until she checked in with her mother from a pay phone on the way.

"I called my mother and she said, 'Are you at that giant thing that's on the TV where everybody is tied up and trying to get into that big concert?'" she said. "I said, 'I don't think so.' We didn't know. We had no idea that it was a big deal."

Adrian Lyss, who was seventeen, went with four other people, but when they hit traffic that was too backed up to move, two of her group left, taking the car with them.

Lyss and her other two friends began walking to the festival grounds. They weren't alone. People were abandoning their cars and trekking to the site on foot, for as far as they could see.

It didn't take long for the people living by the roadside to see an economic opportunity. Residents lined the road to sell sandwiches and water to concertgoers, and when it got dark, Lyss and her friends paid a woman a few bucks to sleep in her basement. After a couple of hours' rest, they kept going.

Twenty-year-old Vince Scarlata, meanwhile, made the very understandable assumption that a festival called "Woodstock" would actually be held in the town of Woodstock, so that's where he went.

"We get downtown and we're saying, 'Where the hell is the venue?'" he said. A passing motorist told him that the festival was actually in Bethel, sixty miles away, and gave them a ride.

"About forty minutes later or so, we come to a dead stop," he said, and he and his friends walked from that point on. "We walked, I don't know, for a couple of hours."

Drew Semon, who was sixteen, didn't reach the festival grounds until dawn on Sunday morning. He said that he and his friend were able to find their way to the site by following their ears. "You could hear the Who just reverberating through the night air," he said.

Jim Mesthene, who was sixteen, hitchhiked with a friend. It was a simple plan, provided you weren't too choosy about riding inside.

"Everyone was riding on the outside of cars," he said. "Just hop on the hood or hop on the trunk or on the roof or something. Often there were ten people riding on, or crammed in, the car."

The best way to get there was by motorcycle, which made it possible to bypass the stopped cars. Jerry Wolfert, who was twenty-four, got there on one and saw a couple on another one.

"A couple went by me, absolutely stark naked," he said, and he watched as they were stopped by a police officer. "The cop said, 'It's illegal in New York State, what you're doing.' They said, 'Why?' and he said, 'We have a helmet law.' So they put helmets on, and the two of them just rode away." ◆

The Traffic

By the time the music started at Woodstock, traffic leading to the site was pretty much at a standstill. To get the performers in and out, the promoters hired helicopters.

"When the world tried to arrive at the same time, we had to change plans and go to helicopters for the most part," Michael Lang said. "It was a more convenient way to get the band members, in any case."

That left the matter of the performers' equipment, which was too heavy to bring on the helicopters, and which had to be transported by trucks.

"That was something that couldn't come by helicopter; it came by road," Lang said. "That was a bit of a struggle. I mean there were back roads that were somewhat free. That's how [Jefferson] Airplane came, that's how some of the acts sort of arrived. That's how a lot of the acts arrived from one of the local motels. So, there were some back roads, but basically helicopters were the method of choice."

The audience, on the other hand, had to deal with the traffic that had backed up for miles. Some resorted to creative methods to get around it.

Gail Hayssen, who was fourteen, said that she and her five friends were driving to the concert from Forest Hills, New York, when they hit traffic that had ground to a halt. "We were determined to get there, so in a spontaneous moment, Ricky drove the yellow Impala in reverse, up an on-ramp, and cut across the freeway."

On August 16, 1969, the headline of the *New York Daily News* read, "Traffic Uptight at Hippie Fest." While the headline and some of the reporting may have reeked of easily discernible *schadenfreude*, you couldn't dispute reporter Joseph Modzelewski's data.

Describing the crowd as "hip and hairy," he called it "the largest traffic jam in the history of the Catskills," and he was right. State police had closed Exit 104, which led to Route 17B, shutting down traffic.

According to state police, traffic was backed up for seventeen miles along Route 17B, the road between Monticello and White Lake. They reported delays of as much as eight hours from New York City to White Lake, normally a ninety-minute drive. An unidentified state trooper made no attempt to dress it up.

"The situation is hopeless and getting worse," he said.

State troopers weren't the only ones describing the situation in grim terms. *Rolling Stone*'s Jan Hodenfield reported that the Short Line, the sole bus line serving the area from New York City, had canceled all service to the area, on the orders of local police. This was fine with Short Line bus drivers, who had in one case taken twelve hours to make the trip.

"We're not driving into that disaster area," a spokesman from Short Line said. ◆

Elliott Landy

Elliott Landy was the official photographer at Woodstock. Prior to the festival, he had worked for underground newspapers, taking pictures of antiwar demonstrations and Fillmore East concerts, either of which would be interesting subjects for most photographers. But Landy needed to connect with his work on a deeper level.

"The concerts at the Fillmore East were like happenings in a new culture," he said. "For me, I was more into trying to change the existing culture, trying to change the way people behaved and thought. So when I was photographing these concerts, it was a form of proselytization, almost."

That's not to say that he didn't love the music. He did, deeply, or he never would have taken the gigs in the first place.

"If I didn't like the music, I was not able to take photographs of the person or band playing," he said. "My inner connection to photographing is so deep that when I don't like something, that connection is switched off and I don't take pictures."

His profile increased significantly when he photographed album covers for two artists who had taken up residence in the town of Woodstock—the Band and Bob Dylan. According to Landy, the covers for *Music from Big Pink* and *Nashville Skyline* helped establish that rural Catskills town as a mecca for the counterculture's music and as a refuge for its most revered artists.

"Dylan was the most famous person in the music world at that time," he said. "And then *Music from Big Pink* came out, and that added to the myth, I guess…my pictures were intrinsically very deeply associated with that mystique."

Landy left Manhattan behind and took up residence in Woodstock, finding much more space in which to work for much less money. It was there that he met promoter Michael Lang.

"I didn't know what he did, but one day he called me and said he wanted to come over to talk," he said. "So he rode up to my house in the woods on his motorcycle, and he said, 'I'm producing a festival; do you want to photograph it?'"

The promoter listed some of the artists who would be performing, and Landy agreed on the spot. But to this day, he maintains that Woodstock was less a music festival than a spiritual event, one intended to teach people how to relate to one another.

"It was about people…becoming what we want the planet to be, which is a loving communal experience where people look out for each other along with taking care of their own needs," he said.

Landy had no crew at Woodstock—just five cameras, two exposure meters, and forty rolls of film. At least one of the cameras, a Widelux panoramic camera, was the state-of-the-art for its time.

"The lens rotates, and I was able to get panoramic shots of the audience," he said. "I

actually have a picture that I took by accident with my panoramic camera under the stage. At the time, I thought it was a wasted shot. I thought it was a waste of film, but now I'm so happy to have that photograph."

Landy was not the only photographer working the festival. He credited Henry Diltz, an accomplished photographer in his own right, whose home address in California prevented him from being part of what Landy called the "Woodstock vibe."

"Not to diminish his role or his pictures certainly," Landy said of Diltz. "He's a great photographer, and a great guy."

There was also Amalie Rothschild, who took one of his favorite pictures of the entire weekend.

"There's a great picture of me," he said. "The photographer is Amalie Rothschild, and it's a beautiful picture of me onstage with all my cameras and exposure meters, and so on."

Landy has since enjoyed a successful career that's gone in many stylistic directions, but demand for his photography from that weekend has never waned. And as much as he enjoys working in other genres and taking on new projects, he doesn't want it to wane.

"I keep doing new things, but I still print the old stuff and I still sell it, and I still am part of it, because I really love it," he said. "It's like a child. You don't stop loving a child because you have new ones. You have more children and keep loving them all." ◆

It's a Free Festival

Carol Clapp was twenty-one when she took a job selling tickets to Woodstock. The promoters had not yet declared the festival free, so the event was still supposed to cost money at that point. She knew how many tickets had been sold, and it was more than anyone had predicted. A lot more.

"I knew it was going to be a bigger deal than we originally thought," she said. "We were on site prior to the beginning of the festival, and we were getting reports about traffic tie-ups. At that point, we knew it was going to be much bigger than we expected."

She was right. At more than 400,000 people, it was a crowd bigger than the population of many US cities. More important, it was a number of people too enormous to politely ask to form an orderly line to buy tickets, and there was no way to keep them out.

Jeffrey Karasik, who was eighteen, said that even if the organizers had decided to keep selling tickets, they would never have been able to keep out people who didn't have them.

"The fences were just snowdrift fences, just little red sticks that were rolled out," he said. "They really weren't much value to anybody who was determined to go into the place."

The promoters decided that rather than fight the escalating situation, they would announce that Woodstock was a free festival. In doing so, they chose the least worst option.

The last-minute venue change had left them without enough time to finish all the necessary construction. They could either finish the stage or finish the fences and ticket booths.

They couldn't do both, and letting thousands of people pay to get in when the stage wasn't finished was an invitation to something much worse than mere financial ruin.

"It was either bankruptcy or a riot," Rosenman told *Newsday* in 2009.

Wavy Gravy said that the Hog Farm helped organizers make the decision to stop selling or collecting tickets. He and Hog Farm member Tom Law were approached by a crew member, who told them that they were about to start taking tickets, and asked if the two of them could clear the infield to make room for this process.

"I looked around and there's about forty thousand people in the infield," he said. "'Do you want a good movie or a bad movie?' he asked the crew member, referring to the *Woodstock* documentary that was to be filmed. He also may have been implying that this was the moment for Woodstock Ventures to decide if they really wanted a disaster on their hands.

Less than fifteen minutes later, Woodstock was declared a free festival.

Carol Clapp said that there was one last thought given to trying to make a little more money, but it was out of the question.

"There was some talk of us going around collecting money in a basket, collecting contributions, and I said, 'No I'm not going to do that in this crowd, I might get ripped apart'," she said.

Many people who had actually bought tickets in advance as they were supposed to were not pleased.

"I paid eighteen dollars and at that time, that's a lot of money," said Vince Scarlata,

who was twenty.

Many people who bought tickets still have them to this day. But there were those who did their best to use them, even after ticket collection was abandoned.

"We put our tickets on the ticket booth like idiots," said Don Stark, who was seventeen. "Like, 'Okay, we're good citizens, here they are.'" ◆

THE FUNNY THING IS,
I GUESS, WHEN THE
RAIN SET IN AND
IT BECAME SORT OF
AWFUL, THE SPIRIT
DIDN'T GET WORSE.

—Ernie Brooks

I SLEPT IN THE RAIN
OR DIDN'T EVEN SLEEP.
I JUST STAYED OUT IN
THE RAIN ALL NIGHT.

—Vince Scarlata

I KIND OF GREW UP WITH THAT WHOLE FIFTIES MENTALITY AND NEVER FIT IN. I ALWAYS FELT REALLY GOOD IN THIS SIXTIES ENVIRONMENT, BUT I WAS ISOLATED. THE MAIN FEELING I HAD AT WOODSTOCK WAS, "OH MY GOD, THERE'S ALL THESE PEOPLE THERE WHO FEEL LIKE I DO," AND I FELT LIKE I WAS IN THIS COMMUNITY, I WASN'T ALONE ANYMORE. I'M ONE OF MANY NOW, AND ALL THESE PEOPLE FEEL LIKE I DO, AND ALL THESE PEOPLE LOVE THIS MUSIC.

—Adrian Lyss

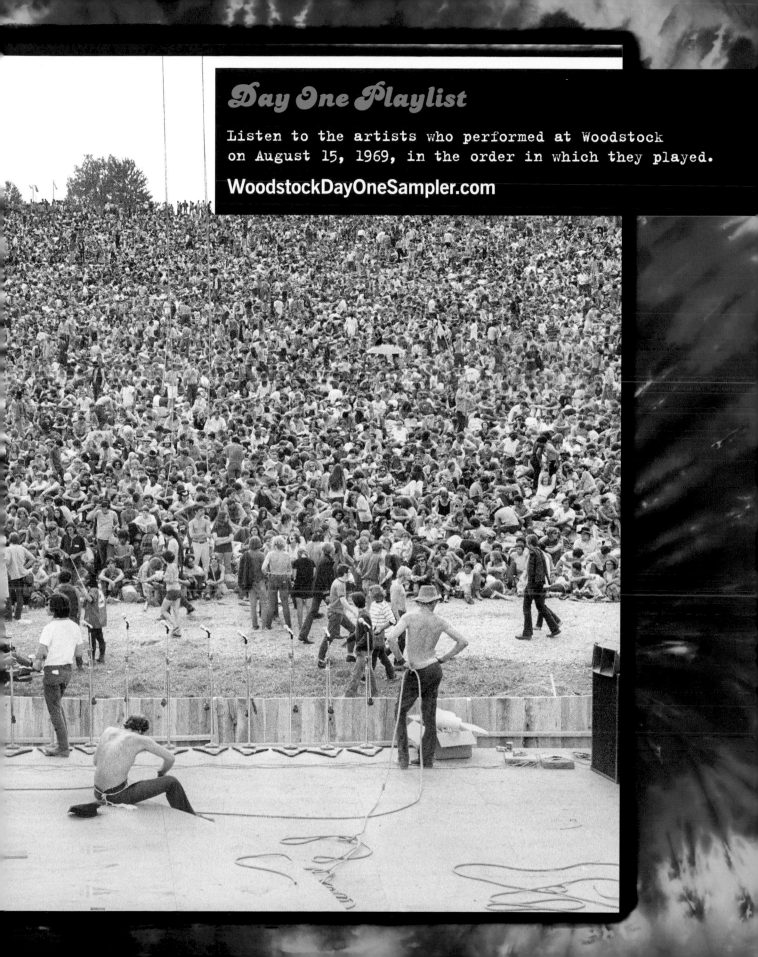

Day One Playlist

Listen to the artists who performed at Woodstock
on August 15, 1969, in the order in which they played.

WoodstockDayOneSampler.com

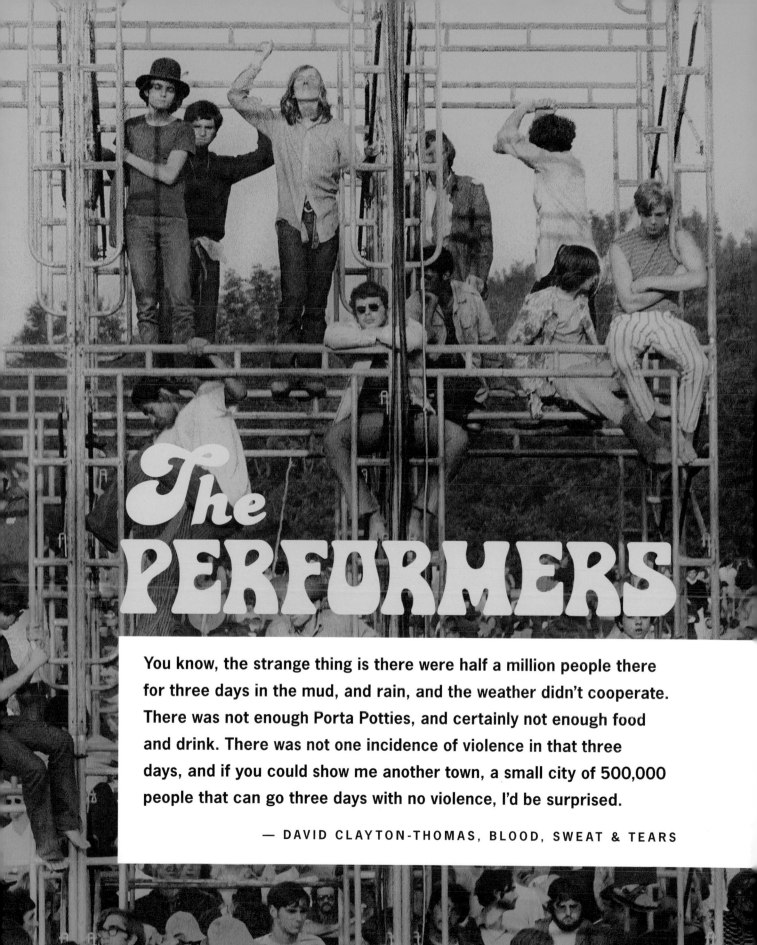

The PERFORMERS

You know, the strange thing is there were half a million people there for three days in the mud, and rain, and the weather didn't cooperate. There was not enough Porta Potties, and certainly not enough food and drink. There was not one incidence of violence in that three days, and if you could show me another town, a small city of 500,000 people that can go three days with no violence, I'd be surprised.

— DAVID CLAYTON-THOMAS, BLOOD, SWEAT & TEARS

Richie Havens

AUGUST 15, 1969

BEFORE WOODSTOCK, RICHIE Havens was an established recording artist with several albums to his credit. Woodstock delineated a dividing line in his career, with one side clearly marked "before" and the other marked "after."

A Brooklyn native, he was part of the burgeoning Greenwich Village folk music scene, where he had been a fixture since his teenage years. When he turned twenty, he became a musician.

"I had first gone there during the beatnik days of the 1950s to perform poetry, then I drew portraits for two years and stayed up all night listening to folk music in the clubs," he said on his website in 2008. "It took a while before I thought of picking up a guitar."

Havens was self-taught and developed a unique style that was equal parts open tuning and forceful strumming. But it was his singing voice, which was somehow both tortured and effortless, that was truly one of a kind.

His third album, *Richard P. Havens, 1983*, was in stores when he performed at Woodstock. Although he famously opened the festival, that wasn't the way it was supposed to work out. That honor was supposed to go to the Los Angeles band Sweetwater, who were stuck in traffic.

"We couldn't get anybody in, so we just had to get people together and get them onstage and start performing," said John Morris. "With Richie, I grabbed him, put him on the stage, and said, 'You've got to play, you've got to play.'"

Havens began just after five o'clock in the afternoon on Friday. In doing so, he not only bought time for the other acts to arrive, but he also unknowingly created what Michael Lang would tell the *Washington Examiner* was his favorite moment of the entire weekend—"when Richie went on and the sound system worked."

As Havens performed, the other acts still hadn't shown up, so he was asked to keep going and going. He did, and he gave it absolutely everything he had. He even performed a few Beatles songs for good measure. After performing eleven songs, he was utterly depleted, but he was also, still, the only performer on the festival grounds.

"You can see in the film, I put my arm

around him, and said, 'You've got to go back and play some more again, there's nobody to put on'," said Morris. "I did that about three times, until he invented the 'Freedom' song."

"Freedom" was a song based on the spiritual "Motherless Child," and while he may have come up with it then and there, it's the song that Havens remained best known for throughout the rest of his career. In a 2008 interview with Cliff Smith of Music-News.com, he said that the song was born out of pure necessity.

"I'd already played every song I knew, and I was stalling, asking for more guitar and mic, trying to think of something else to play—and then it just came to me."

After the song was finished, he left the Woodstock stage for good. John Morris said that there was nothing more he could ask of the performer at that point, and he was right.

"After that, he was soaking wet," Morris said. "He came off and he said, 'I can't do it, man. I'm done. I've given it.' I said, 'Yeah, you're out. Thank you. God bless you.'"

His appearance was featured in the *Woodstock* documentary, which gave an enormous boost to his career. According to Artie Kornfeld, Havens never actually wanted to be in the movie in the first place, and he had to be filmed without his knowledge.

"Richie didn't want to do the movie," he said. "And that's why all the shots of Richie are looking up his nose, because they were shooting him illegally from his hip. Richie couldn't even see the camera was there."

Havens remained an active musician for the rest of his life, until he stopped touring in

2012 for health reasons. In April 2013, he passed away from a heart attack at the age of seventy-two. He had his ashes scattered at the festival site, where his marathon performance had transformed his career.

"What an incredible job he did," said Kornfeld. "He sang for an hour and forty-five minutes, and he didn't expect to be up there." ◆

I'd already played every song I knew, and I was stalling, asking for more guitar and mic, trying to think of something else to play—and then ["Freedom"] just came to me.
—RICHIE HAVENS

Swami Satchidananda

AUGUST 15, 1969

Swami Satchidananda was an Indian yogi and religious instructor who gave the opening invocation at Woodstock, after the first two artists had performed.

Born in 1914 as Ramaswamy Gounder, he originally worked in his family's automobile import business, according to *The New York Times*. Five years after marrying, his wife passed away, and he shifted his focus from business to spirituality.

In 1949, he met his guru, H. H. Sri Swami Sivananda, and was initiated into monkhood, given the name Swami Satchidananda, and sent to serve in other parts of India and Sri Lanka.

The psychedelic artist Peter Max brought him to the United States in 1966. The timing couldn't have been better. An infatuation with Indian music and meditation had taken hold in

the West, and Satchidananda was now perfectly positioned to spread his influence.

Satchidananda was embraced by the counterculture, whose adherents were tuning in, turning on, and dropping out. He interpreted their drug use as symptomatic of a quest for something bigger and more meaningful than their daily lives could provide.

"They are all searching for the necklace that's around their necks," he said, according to the book, *Back to the Garden: The Story of Woodstock*. "Eventually they'll look in the mirror and see it."

In the years following Woodstock, he founded six yoga centers in the United States, including one in Buckingham County, Virginia, that sat on 750 acres of woodland. He died in 2002 at the age of eighty-seven while attending a peace conference in Madras, South India. ◆

Sweetwater

AUGUST 15, 1969

SET LIST

Motherless Child / Look Out /

For Pete's Sake / Day Song

What's Wrong / Crystal Spider

Two Worlds / Why Oh Why

Let the Sunshine In / Oh Happy Day

SWEETWATER WAS THE FIRST FULL band to perform at Woodstock. They were supposed to open the festival, but they were stuck in the famously impassable traffic, so their slot went to Richie Havens. They ultimately reached the festival grounds via one of the sixteen helicopters that Woodstock Ventures had hired to bypass the traffic.

The group was frequently compared to Jefferson Airplane, in all likelihood because their lead singer, Nancy Nevins, was a woman. But the two groups sounded nothing alike. They used unusual instrumentation, such as cello and flute, and placed very little emphasis on the guitar.

The band was managed by Bruce Glatman, and having him in their corner proved to be a boon. Not only was he friends with Bill Graham, but according to John Morris, he had the necessary tenacity to get them the gig.

"Sweetwater was a band that I wanted to put on because Bruce Glatman, their manager, was driving me crazy," he said.

While Glatman may have been aware of the significance of the gig, Nevins said that she and the rest of the band weren't. When they got there, all they knew was that they were contending with major technical problems in front of the largest audience they had ever seen.

"The sound system wasn't working yet, and the plywood stage wobbled, maybe from having just been built," she said. "There were no vocal monitors, and all the instruments fed through the four standing vocal mics."

It wasn't until they returned to Los Angeles and saw the coverage on television that they began to understand the significance of the festival. Unfortunately, it didn't do them much good.

"Sweetwater did a great performance," Michael Lang said. "Their career just never really took off. I think they had a decent following, but you know, in that context, they really didn't cut through. So, what can you say? They were a great band, but they just didn't make a big impression."

Sweetwater's career was dealt a death blow just after Woodstock when Nevins, then just twenty years old, was in a major car accident. She was in a coma for ten days, suffered damage to her vocal cords, and required intensive physical therapy for years afterward. In her absence, the band stopped touring. They also weren't featured in either the *Woodstock* documentary or on the soundtrack album. The band broke up in 1971.

Flautist Albert Moore of Woodstock's scheduled opening act, the Los Angeles band Sweetwater.

Sweetwater made its first attempt at a reunion in 1994. Cellist August Burns, drummer Alan Malarowitz, and flautist Albert Moore had all passed away by then, and conga player Elpidio "Pete" Cobian had left the music industry. This left only Nevins, keyboard player Alex Del Zoppo, and bassist Fred Herrera to represent the original band.

In 1999, VH1 released the movie *Sweetwater: A True Rock Story*, which told the story of the group. It starred Amy Jo Johnson, of the WB series *Felicity*, as the twenty-year-old version of Nancy Nevins and Michelle Phillips, of the Mamas and the Papas, as the grown-up version.

Despite the ups and downs that Nevins experienced, she said that she was just happy to have been at Woodstock, even if it didn't catapult the group to superstardom.

"I'm grateful to my toes to have been part of 1960s music....Those were creative and stimulating days." ◆

> *I'm grateful to my toes to have been part of 1960s music....Those were creative and stimulating days.*
>
> **—NANCY NEVINS**

Bert Sommer

AUGUST 15, 1969

SET LIST

Jennifer / The Road to Travel /

I Wondered Where You'd Be /

She's Gone / Things Are Going My Way /

And When It's Over / Jeanette /

America / A Note That Read / Smile

BERT SOMMER, THE FOURTH ACT to perform at Woodstock, remains obscure to this day, despite appearing before thousands of people at an event that's still famous half a century later.

It wasn't because of his performance. YouTube is full of footage that attests to its pristine grace. The audience loved him, too.

Artie Kornfeld had signed him to Capitol Records, and he booked him at Woodstock. He had high praise for him and regards it as a shame that he was never better known.

"He's the one that got away," he said. "He's probably the most talented artist, including the Beatles, that I've ever been involved with. He wrote incredible. He was so easy. I never had to do more than one vocal

with Bert. In the studio, you know, he stayed simple. He listened to me. There were no ego trips between us at all. I looked at him like he was a kid brother."

His career began in 1967, when he joined the New York City pop group the Left Banke.

"Working with Bert was truly like working with a genius," Left Banke keyboard player Michael Brown said on Sommer's tribute website. "Bert taught himself everything. He would play piano without thumbs early on, just four fingers on each hand. We wrote many songs together and I also had a great time playing with him live onstage in his early career."

After Sommer was cast in the Broadway musical *Hair*, Kornfeld signed him to Capitol Records, which released his debut album, *The Road to Travel*, in 1968.

"I promised Bert that I was going to get him there and people were going to hear him," Kornfeld told the *Wall Street Journal* in 2009. "Bert seemed to be born knowing how to write. His music blew me away. I liked his style and his sincerity."

Sommer performed a ten-song set at Woodstock just before sunset. He didn't appear either in the *Woodstock* documentary or on the soundtrack album.

It's hard to know how much damage that did to Sommer's career, but Kornfeld told the *Wall Street Journal* that had he appeared in the film and on the soundtrack, "it would have been instant stardom for him."

Michael Lang agreed.

"Had he not been cut, I think he would have had a huge career," he said. According to those who knew him, Sommer was deeply wounded by his omission from the movie and soundtrack.

"He was devastated," said Victor Kahn, a personal friend who spoke with the *Wall Street Journal*. "Here was the most famous event in the world and he's not getting any credit for it."

Sommer pressed on with his career, releasing three more albums. He was also a member of Kaptain Kool and the Kongs, a fictional band that existed only to host *The Krofft Supershow*, a children's television program that featured the superhero exploits of Electra Woman and Dyna Girl.

Sommer died of respiratory failure in 1990 at the age of forty-one. For those who knew him, it's more than just his music that they miss.

He's the one that got away. He's probably the most talented artist, including the Beatles, that I've ever been involved with.

—ARTIE KORNFELD

"A remarkable person," said Michael Brown on Sommer's memorial website. "Most of all, he was a good friend. We all miss him." ◆

Tim Hardin

AUGUST 15, 1969

How Can We Hang on to a Dream? /

Susan / If I Were a Carpenter /

Reason to Believe / You Upset the

Grace of Living When You Lie /

Speak Like a Child / Snow White Lady

Blue on My Ceiling / Simple Song of

Freedom / Misty Roses

EVEN IF YOU DON'T KNOW TIM Hardin's name, you know at least one song that he wrote.

His career as a singer and songwriter never reached great commercial heights, and he died in obscurity. But he wrote songs that became hits for other artists and which have remained favorites for the last half-century.

These include "If I Were a Carpenter," which was recorded by fellow Woodstock alumnus Joan Baez, and "Reason to Believe," which was a hit for Rod Stewart twice, both in 1971 and in a newly recorded *Unplugged* version in 1993. His songs were also covered by a range of artists across different styles, including Johnny Cash and Astrud Gilberto.

Unfortunately, Hardin's own career was hampered by drug abuse, and a heroin over-dose cut his life short before he even reached the age of forty.

An Oregon native, Hardin dropped out of high school at age eighteen and enlisted in the Marines. It was during his tour of duty that he discovered heroin, buying so much of it during a stint in Hong Kong that he had enough to last him for most of his two-year deployment.

He was discharged in 1961, and after a period performing around Greenwich Village, he relocated to Boston and became a regular on the city's folk music circuit. After a false start on Columbia Records that saw his first recordings shelved, he signed to Verve Forecast.

His debut, *Tim Hardin 1*, featured string overdubs that did the material no favors, and which Hardin himself objected to, according to AllMusic.com. Nonetheless, it got some airplay and positioned him well for his next album, *Tim Hardin 2*.

Hardin's sophomore outing is considered by many to be his finest. It kicks off with "If I Were a Carpenter," which became a top ten hit for Bobby Darin in both the United States and the United Kingdom.

Unfortunately, due to a mixture of drug abuse and poor health, Hardin was never able to build on its success. He contracted a viral

perform at Woodstock. Apart from being a fan of his music, he also said that he wanted to give the musician a leg up when he really seemed to need one. Unfortunately, it didn't do the trick.

"Tim was a friend of mine," he said. "I was hoping this was going to be a big comeback for him, but he was involved with heroin and just was not up to the show."

The Woodstock set did not appear either in the movie or on the original soundtrack

lung infection in 1968 and canceled an English tour that same year, after falling asleep onstage at the Royal Albert Hall, according to *The Rough Guide to Rock*.

Despite Hardin's career being on a downswing, Michael Lang wanted him to

album, and despite Lang's hopes of helping him revive a flagging career, Hardin's problems only worsened. He would release just three more albums in his lifetime, the last being 1973's *Nine*. He died from a heroin overdose in 1980. ◆

Ravi Shankar

AUGUST 15, 1969

RAVI SHANKAR WAS AN UNEQUALED master of the sitar. To this day, he remains one of the only Indian musicians that Western audiences know by name.

His career began during the 1940s, after years of studying Hindustani classical music. Starting in 1949, he composed scores for Indian films, but when he met the Beatles' George Harrison in London in 1966, everything changed.

Harrison was already enamored with Indian music—so much so that he had played the sitar on the song "Norwegian Wood (This Bird Has Flown)." However, Shankar taught him the right way to sit with the instrument and play it properly.

Although Harrison refused to take credit for it, Shankar's association with him increased the Indian musician's profile in the West considerably. Now he would be embraced by audiences in the hippie counterculture, whether he wanted to be or not.

Shankar's first experience with rock festivals was in 1967, when he performed at Monterey Pop. He kept his mouth shut at the time, but thirty years later, he revealed to *Rolling Stone* that his response to Jimi Hendrix's performance was one of horror.

"I saw how wonderful he was at the guitar, and I was really admiring him, and then he started his antics," he told *Rolling Stone*. "Making love to the guitar. And then, as if that was not enough, he burned the guitar. That was too much for me. In our culture, we have such respect for musical instruments, they are like part of God."

Appalled though he may have been, he agreed to play at Woodstock, his second rock festival appearance and, ironically, his second time sharing a bill with Jimi Hendrix. His performance did not appear in the *Woodstock* documentary, a decision that technical director Chris Langhart laid squarely at the feet of Shankar's manager.

"His manager barged into the tent, and told [recording engineer Lee] Osborne, 'Give me the tape'," Langhart said. "I'm sure that [Warner Bros.] would have been pleased to have it used [in the *Woodstock* documentary], but without the sound, they couldn't do a thing about it."

tion that Dr. Timothy Leary and others were propagating—that everyone in India takes drugs," he told the *Guardian* in 2008. "It was a hodgepodge of *Kama Sutra*, Tantra, yoga, hash, and LSD, while the true spiritual quality of our music was almost completely lost."

Shankar's relationship with Harrison, meanwhile, never wavered. In 1971, the former Beatle helped his friend organize The Concert for Bangladesh, a benefit at Madison Square Garden that saw such superstars as Bob Dylan and Eric Clapton lend a hand to fund relief efforts for Bangladeshi refugees.

When Harrison died in 2001, Shankar performed at The Concert for George, a 2002 memorial for his friend. The proceeds went to the Material World Charitable Foundation, which the former Beatle had organized in 1973 "to encourage the

Despite the fact that Western audiences embraced him, Shankar was never able to reconcile the hippie culture's appetite for drugs with his own religious beliefs.

"I was extremely unhappy about the superficiality of it all, especially the wrong informa-

exploration of alternate and diverse forms of artistic expression, life views, and philosophies as well as a way to support established charities and people with special needs," according to its website. Shankar died in 2012 at the age of ninety-two. ◆

Melanie plays
for an audience
one thousand
times larger
than the
largest audi-
ence she had
ever played for
previously.

Melanie

AUGUST 15, 1969

MELANIE, WHOSE FULL NAME IS MELANIE SAFKA, performed at Woodstock on Friday, August 15. She had released one album, 1968's *Born to Be*.

Peter Schekeryk, her manager and future husband, had an office at 1650 Broadway in Manhattan, where the Woodstock promoters also had one. He got her a meeting with them, and Artie Kornfeld booked her.

She still lived with her parents in Queens and described herself at the time as not especially gregarious. Nonetheless, she traveled into Manhattan regularly to perform on the sidewalk for strangers, and whenever she did, the shyness and stage fright evaporated.

"I'd go in with my guitar strapped to my back," she said. "Once I start singing, I am who I am, and all of that nonsense disappears."

Melanie's song "Beautiful People" was in heavy rotation with underground disc jockeys, and the biggest crowd that she had ever played for was five hundred people. She had no idea that she had agreed to play for almost a thousand times that many people.

"I just thought it was going to be a picnic in the park," she said. "You know, the hill, on a farm, and it was going to be everyone on picnic blankets, and families."

She drove to Woodstock with her mother, and as they got closer, they hit a snarl of traffic that stretched for miles. She thought they had just run into some congestion, and she didn't put two and two together until they reached their hotel.

"Everybody was meeting at this hotel," she said, referring to a nearby Holiday Inn. "And [in] the other part of the lobby is Janis Joplin, surrounded by microphones and media, and she's slugging Southern Comfort."

While some might have been excited at the opportunity to be in such a celebrity-laden setting, Melanie said that her reaction was exactly the opposite.

"It was just unbelievable that it was me in this situation," she said. "I'm me, just me, and no percussionist, no bass player, no manager, no one to put me in the right places, just me, and again, I'm an introvert. All I wanted to do was get out of there."

Melanie was brought to the festival site by helicopter. It was the first time she had ever been inside one. It might have been easier if she had had her mother there, but her mother had been forbidden to get in with her. She arrived completely alone, and then retreated to a tent in what she called "the folkie area."

"Sorry, mom, bye mom," she said. "This is just for artists, managers. You know, I was just in this whirlwind of 'what the hell?' and I get into the helicopter. I say goodbye to my mother and I didn't see her ever again until way late."

She said that people have always assumed that she must have hobnobbed and rubbed elbows with fabulous celebrities at Woodstock, but it wasn't so.

"Everyone always thinks, 'Oh you must have had a lot of fun hanging out with Janis Joplin and three hundred characters,'" she said. In fact, the only interaction she had with anybody during the long hours in which she waited to go on was when someone would come into the tent and say, "You're on next," which was a false alarm the first several times it happened.

At one point, she thought that rain might bring her a reprieve.

"It was raining, and I began thinking, 'Oh, this is great, all these people will go home!'" she said. "I really, really thought everyone is going to leave now, because it's raining, and sensible people wouldn't be staying there."

Eventually, she was told she was on next, and this time it was the real thing. She got onstage, approached the microphone, and had what she described as an out-of-body experience.

"I wasn't drug-altered, but something happened," she said. "I guess it was a protective mechanism, you know? I wasn't with my body anymore."

She looked out into the crowd and saw thousands of people holding lit candles, which had been distributed by the Hog Farm. At that point, all the fear that had built up in her before the performance melted away. She had a new audience ritual in place, too.

"People would come to my shows after that in New York and then it grew to other places, and they'd bring candles or lighters to signify that they were there," she said. "And then, when I wrote a song called 'Candle in the Rain', it was all over, and it was the thing you do at a Melanie show."

After Woodstock, people would light candles whenever she performed the song. This led some venues to force her to sign papers agreeing not to perform it, or she would hear from the fire marshals.

Because she's still an active, touring musician today, one can safely say that it didn't hold her back.

"I was never afraid again on stage," she said. "I was free to do what I wanted." ◆

Arlo Guthrie

AUGUST 15, 1969

*A*RLO GUTHRIE IS A DIRECT descendant of folkie royalty. His father was Woody Guthrie, the man who wrote "This Land Is Your Land," and who remains one of the most significant artists in the history of American music.

It was a long shadow to grow up under, but Arlo Guthrie never seemed intimidated by it. He carved out his own niche, and he did it with the first song on his first album.

The song, "Alice's Restaurant Massacree," was over eighteen minutes long and took up the entire first side of 1967's *Alice's Restaurant*, his debut. Consisting of a shaggy-dog account of a man receiving a littering citation, it should have sunk from the charts like a rock. Instead, it became his most famous song.

Guthrie was born in the Coney Island section of Brooklyn. His father hailed from the heartland, his mother, Marjorie Mazia, was Jewish, and raised her son Jewish.

He received his religious training from a rabbi named Meir Kahane, who would go on to found the Jewish Defense League, which the FBI would classify as an extremist group when two of its members planned an attack on a California mosque and the office of US Congressman Darrell Issa in 2001.

"Rabbi Kahane was a really nice, patient teacher, but shortly after he gave me my lessons, he started going haywire," Guthrie said in a 2004 interview with the *Jewish Journal*. "Maybe I was responsible."

After high school, Guthrie traveled to London "for no particular reason except to be there," according to the *People's Daily Morning Star*. He met journalist Karl Dallas, who introduced him to the city's folk scene.

The experience aligned perfectly with the events of Thanksgiving 1965. Now back in the United States, Guthrie threw a load of garbage down a hillside in Stockbridge, Massachusetts, with a friend, an incident detailed in the November 29, 1965, issue of the *Berkshire Eagle*. They pleaded guilty to illegally disposing of rubbish, were fined twenty-five dollars each, and ordered to clean it up.

Arlo Guthrie erroneously told the crowd that the New York State Thruway was closed, even though it wasn't, man.

This extremely minor event provided the genesis for "Alice's Restaurant Massacree." WBAI radio host Bob Fass obtained a recording of an early version of it and played it repeatedly, leading audiences to request it wherever Guthrie performed, according to the book *Something in the Air: Radio, Rock, and the Revolution That Shaped a Generation*.

Guthrie took the stage at Woodstock just before midnight, but he didn't play his most famous song. Instead, he performed spirituals, hymns, and "Coming into Los Angeles," which appeared on the soundtrack album and which provided the music during a montage in the *Woodstock* documentary featuring many people smoking lots and lots of pot through various joints, jays, doobies, and other combustible contraptions.

He also contributed an iconic moment when he announced from the stage that "the New York State Thruway is closed, man." In reality, it was never closed. Traffic was a colossal, well-documented nightmare, but the Thruway itself remained open.

Today, Guthrie remains a popular solo act, but in 2009, he told *The New York Times* that at the performance that he had coming up, he would not play his most famous song.

"Performing it is like being in the same half-hour *Groundhog Day* movie every night of your life," he said. "Most of the audience that follows me is already sick of hearing of it." ◆

Joan Baez

AUGUST 15, 1969

JOAN BAEZ WAS THE LAST ACT TO PERFORM AT WOODSTOCK on Friday, August 15. According to almost everyone who saw her, she was the perfect person for the job.

"We could not have closed and put everybody to bed the first night as well if we didn't have Joan Baez," said John Morris. "Joan was the perfect sort of lullaby that let everybody be calm and go to sleep."

Born in Staten Island, New York, Baez began performing professionally in 1958, when she was seventeen years old. Her father had taken a job at the Massachusetts Institute of Technology with the family in tow, and this put her right near the flourishing folk music scenes of Boston and Cambridge. According to her memoir, she performed twice a week at Cambridge's Club 47, for twenty-five dollars a night.

She soon met folk singer Bob Gibson, who was so taken with her instantly identifiable voice that he asked her to perform with him at the 1959 Newport Folk Festival. She did, and when she went back to Club 47 for her regular gig, there was a line to see her that stretched around the corner, and then around the next corner. She released her self-titled Vanguard Records debut the following year.

Joan Baez performs "Drug Store Truck Drivin' Man" with singer and guitarist Jeffrey Shurtleff.

Her debut and the follow-up, 1961's *Joan Baez, Vol. 2*, both went gold, and she remained a consistently popular artist throughout the 1960s. By the decade's end, she was a fully established star, and a natural choice to close the first night.

At Woodstock, she was six months pregnant with her son, Gabriel. Taking the stage at one o'clock in the morning, she greeted the crowd with "Good morning," and then started her set. After her third song, "I Shall Be Released," she told the story of her then-husband, David Harris, being taken into custody for draft evasion.

By many accounts, she did more than just perform. She was a stabilizing influence, projecting a calm that made the crowd's mood a little less uneasy.

"That first night was tense," said audience member Dan Mouer, who was twenty-five. "The rain, the crowds, the mud, the disorganization…folks were anxious to say the least. Many were even more anxious than they might have been because they were stoned or tripping. Joan stayed on stage long past her original performance. Just soothing the crowd, talking to everyone, playing her familiar music. She was a beautiful star of that festival."

Baez's warmth wasn't something she reserved only for audiences.

"I developed this deep, bronchial cough," Melanie said. "I guess Joan Baez had heard me coughing and she sent over her personal assistant. She thought, 'Maybe she'd like this?' It was catnip tea with honey and lemon."

Baez closed her set with "We Shall Overcome," and as she left the stage, the light drizzle that had plagued her performance turned

> *Joan stayed on stage long past her original performance. Just soothing the crowd, talking to everyone, playing her familiar music. She was a beautiful star of that festival.*
>
> —DAN MOUER

into a full-fledged downpour. It would get worse as the weekend went on.

Joan Baez remained a committed political activist in the years that followed the festival, and she remained a vital artist for the remainder of her career. In the new millennium, she demonstrated that she would not be pigeonholed as some dusty fossil of the hippie era when she released 2003's *Dark Chords on a Big Guitar*. It was the most "rock" album of her entire career, consisting of songs written by Ryan Adams, Natalie Merchant, Steve Earle, and many others young enough to have been influenced by her.

In 2017, the same year that she was inducted into the Rock and Roll Hall of Fame, she announced her plan to retire from formal touring at the end of 2018. She told *Variety* that she was looking forward to it, now that singing didn't come to her as effortlessly as it used to.

"The voice is so difficult to deal with now that having a point where I don't have to do it anymore will be wonderful," she said.

She also had some choice words for today's aspiring lefties, whom she characterized as too timid to get the job done.

"The liberals are just not smart enough to know how to talk," she said. "For instance, [Nancy] Pelosi, in [referencing] a bill Democrats wanted passed, will say, 'All we were asking is…' You can't say that. 'We are demanding' or 'We are calling for.'…'All we are asking'—it ain't gonna work." ◆

Joan Baez (left, back to camera) enjoys the Woodstock Music & Art Fair with more than 400,000 friends.

First Aid

Although Woodstock was an almost entirely peaceful event, it's not accurate to say that nobody got hurt. In a crowd that size, someone's going to get hurt. It's inevitable.

One of the factors was the rain. *The New York Times* said that staff doctors on site reported an increased threat of bronchial disease and influenza. This was a particular threat to those who wandered naked through the weekend's rainstorms.

The helicopters hired by Woodstock Ventures helped get medical attention to the people who needed it. *The New York Times* reported that they took three people to the Middletown hospital who were in critical condition. Two of them, eighteen-year-old Anthony Gencarelli and twenty-two-year-old Arkie Melunow, had suffered drug overdoses, while eighteen-year-old George Xikis suffered a fractured skull when he fell off of a car roof while intoxicated.

The festival had a first aid tent to treat those who didn't need to be taken to a hospital.

"It was like a *M*A*S*H** tent," said Carol Clapp, who had been hired by Woodstock Ventures to sell tickets to the event. "There were medical professionals there with Thorazine. It brought you down, it counteracted some bad acid or bad mescaline."

Rolling Stone said that five thousand people were ultimately treated, thanks in part to the armed forces. Air Force helicopters brought the more serious cases to an emergency facility in Monticello, and brought back 1,300 pounds of food while they were at it. In all, fifty doctors were airlifted onto the festival grounds to provide first aid.

Dr. William Abruzzi, a local general practitioner, had been hired to oversee emergency medical services. According to the *Journal of*

Emergency Medical Services, he brought on a staff of eighteen physicians, thirty-six nurses, and twenty-seven medical assistants, who worked in eight-hour shifts in trailers and in a thirty-bed hospital tent. At least two doctors and four nurses were always on duty.

The most common problem was cut feet. Many of the concertgoers were barefoot and got cut on broken glass or jagged rocks. Because the festival took place on a farm, the risk of tetanus—caused by the bacterium *Clostridium tetani*, found in soil and manure—was very real.

As a result, on-site medical providers spent a lot of time cleaning and disinfecting cut feet and giving tetanus shots to anyone they treated.

When the festival was over, Abruzzi listed a total of 938 foot lacerations, 23 epileptic seizures, and 176 cases of asthma. He characterized the crowd as well behaved and peaceful.

"There has been no violence whatsoever, which is remarkable for a crowd of this size," he said. ◆

The Brown Acid

Many of the pop culture touchstones that emerged after Woodstock had nothing to do with the music. One came in the form of an announcement that Chip Monck made.

"To get back to the warning that I've received, you may take it with however many grains of salt you wish, that the brown acid that is circulating around us is not specifically too good," he said. "It's suggested that you do stay away from that. Of course, it's your own trip, so be my guest. But please be advised that there's a warning on that one, okay?"

The inclusion of this warning on the Woodstock soundtrack album guaranteed its permanent place in pop culture history. But its substance remains a mystery because no one seems to know what was wrong with the brown acid.

One person who would have seen its effects firsthand was Wavy Gravy, who worked the Freak-Out Tent and saw adverse reactions to LSD all weekend. He said that there would have been no way to tell which acid caused what reaction, just because there was so much of it going around.

"There were about eight hundred different colors of acid," he said.

Michael Lang, on the other hand, said that he knew about the brown acid while the festival was in progress, and he had a sensible, if unspectacular, take on what might have been wrong with it.

"I think it was cut with speed," he said. "It became much more common to have those weird things mixed in with your acid after, in the early seventies. It was kind of rare to have things like speed marketed as any particular acid back then. So that was really it—it wasn't poisonous or anything."

An attendee indentifying as L. Broido, who was familiar with psychedelic drugs at the time, said that not only did he never see any brown acid, but he thought the whole thing was just a rumor that had gotten out of hand.

"I think someone took some acid and freaked out," he said. "Then maybe his buddy freaked out watching him freak out, and they went to the tent, and they said, 'What color?' and it was brown acid. So I

think it just snowballed that way. But I've never seen brown acid, to be honest. I saw a lot of LSD, but I never saw the color brown."

There likely will never be a definitive answer to the question of what, specifically, was wrong with the drug, if it even existed in the first place. The person who manufactured it has never been identified, and the people who ingested it are the stuff of unattributed, anecdotal sources that may or may not be true. Still, based on the information that's out there, one can make a few educated guesses.

One explanation for the effects of the brown acid is a novel one—it may have been too good. The Erowid Center, which describes itself as a nonprofit organization dedicated to recording and preserving reliable information about psychoactive plants and drugs, featured on its website the recollections of a user named "Ocrocker," who claims to have given away several hits of that acid in Max Yasgur's field.

"The truth is that the only problem with the brown acid is that it was so pure that it wasn't accompanied by the usual body rushes caused by speed and other adulterants in use at the time," he said. "As a result, multiple doses of acid that was very strong to begin with were sometimes taken, and some trips got way out of hand."

Without these initial "body rushes" normally associated with the first hour after ingestion, there would have been no way of knowing that the trip was coming on. It's easy to imagine someone taking the drug for the first time and being overwhelmed by the experience if there were no physical indications of its effects kicking in.

Ocrocker said that he gave away several tabs in exchange for food and wine, and he warned the people that he gave it to not to take more than half a tab and not to respond to the lack of body rushes by taking more. Whether they listened or not, nobody can say for sure. Also, nobody can say for sure whether any of this really happened.

No matter what the chemical makeup of the brown acid was, and no matter the story behind it, all sources seem to agree that it caused a strong reaction that simply may have been more than some users were ready for. Whatever the case, Monck's warning gave people who missed the festival some additional insight into what those three days were like—perhaps even more so than the music or the anecdotes. ◆

  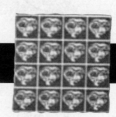 

YASGUR'S FARM WAS LITERALLY
TWO FARMS OVER FROM MY
FAMILY'S FARM, AND I THINK IT WAS
AN ISSUE OF THIS ONE GUY DOING
SOMETHING THAT HAD ENORMOUS
LOCAL IMPACT ON THE COMMUNITY.
IT WAS A HUGE WEEKEND FOR
VEGETABLE SALES, AND NO ONE
COULD GET TO ANY OF THEIR FARMS,
AND THEIR TRUCKS COULD NOT PICK
UP OR DELIVER BECAUSE THE ROADS
WERE FULL OF CARS THAT PEOPLE
HAD PARKED AND JUST LEFT THERE.

—Amanda Bennett, local resident

Food

In his book, *The Road to Woodstock*, Michael Lang described the difficult process of trying to find a food vendor for the festival.

"The large food-vending companies like Restaurant Associates, which handled ballparks and arenas, didn't want to take on Woodstock," he wrote. "No one had ever handled food services for an event this size."

According to *Smithsonian* magazine, the promoters wanted Coney Island's legendary Nathan's to sell hot dogs, but when the venue moved from the town of Woodstock to Sullivan County, they weren't interested. The promoters finally hired Food for Love, a company consisting of exactly three people.

It was woefully inadequate, and many people ate next to nothing the entire time they were there.

"People were taking corn from Yasgur's cornfield," said attendee Vince Scarlata, who was twenty. "People were going in there, taking the corn and eating right off the cob, uncooked, they were so hungry."

Adrian Lyss, who was seventeen, had only the food she brought with her, which wasn't much, but she remembered that whatever people had, they shared.

"I had a couple of sandwiches with me, and I remember I had shared that," she said. "Everybody passed around and shared what they had."

The Food for Love concessions were quickly swamped, and Lang said that they responded to the long lines and dwindling supplies by quadrupling their prices. Angry festivalgoers responded by setting two of the concession stands on fire.

The Hog Farm diffused the situation. The promoters had allowed them to run a free kitchen on the grounds, which served brown rice, vegetables, and a new concoction called "granola." They never charged a cent.

John Morris credited the Hog Farm's Lisa Law with predicting the shortages and suggesting that a free kitchen be set up to compensate.

"They fed a quarter million people throughout the festival," he said. "They just realized there was going to be a problem and they would help solve it, and they did."

When the food was ready, Wavy Gravy made an announcement that was later called one of the top entertainment lines of the twentieth century by *Entertainment Weekly*.

"What we have in mind is breakfast in bed for 100,000," he announced from the stage.

Jim Mesthene, who was sixteen, had no problem finding food. Trucks carrying produce had been diverted to the festival site, and he and fifteen other people spent most of the weekend in the back of a banana truck.

"We spent all our time there sitting on bananas, eating bananas, handing out bananas," he said. "I have never eaten a banana since." ◆

Where's the Bathroom?

If Woodstock attendees had one major complaint—apart from the rain, mud, and lack of food—it was the bathroom situation. Put simply, there weren't enough of them.

"We only had 1,500 toilets," John Morris said. "But they were the 1,500 that made the deal. Somebody said, 'You should get 5,000 or more toilets.' But A, I doubt we could have found them, and B, we wouldn't have thought it made sense."

If Morris's recollection is correct, there were 1,500 toilets for more than 400,000 people, which means that there was one toilet for every 267 concertgoers. If they had been in perfect working condition, that would have made the situation marginally better, but according to *Rolling Stone,* no such luck.

"The sanitation facilities…were breaking down and overflowing," *Rolling Stone*'s Jan Hodenfield reported. "The water from six wells and parked water tanks were proving to be an inadequate supply for the long lines that were forming, and the aboveground water pipes were being crushed by the humanity."

Some of those who used the toilets were too traumatized by them to do so twice.

"I only went to the bathroom once that I can remember," said attendee JoAnn Devitt. "I didn't drink anything because I didn't want to have to go back in there."

Another audience member, Marla Argintar, wasn't put off by the relative lack of facilities, but she described herself as an outdoors type.

"You just went in the woods," she said. "I mean, it was no big deal."

Some never saw a single toilet the entire weekend.

"I never even saw where the Porta-Potties were," said Adrian Lyss. "We would just go to the side where the trees were to go to the bathroom."

Gerry Swislow, who was seventeen, dealt with the situation the same way any self-respecting, grossed-out teenager deals with the uncomfortable subject of number two.

"I would guess that I probably didn't shit the whole time," he said.

Jack Deacy, who covered Woodstock for the *New York Daily News*, was blunt.

"People were pissing and shitting all over the place," he said. "There were definitely people who were relieving themselves because they didn't want to wait in line for fifteen to twenty minutes."

There was at least one person who tried to make the portable toilet experience more agreeable for those who could get to one. His name was Tom Taggart, and he appears in the *Woodstock* documentary, cleaning the Port-O-San facilities.

A bald, stout man of middle age, he comes across as genial and happy to be doing his job. He said that one of his own sons was there that day, while another was in Vietnam. It's a jarring scene, if only because it's a reminder that even in the Garden of Eden, someone has to scrub the toilets.

Taggart sued the makers of the *Woodstock* documentary for using the footage in which he appears. The lawsuit was denied in 1974. ◆

ALMOST EVERYBODY WHO WAS THERE WERE PEACEFUL PEOPLE WHO CARED ABOUT PEACE AND LOVE, AND THAT'S WHAT THEY EXPECTED. PEOPLE WERE JUST VERY MELLOW AND VERY CHILL ABOUT THE WHOLE THING. THERE WEREN'T A LOT OF REDNECKS, THOSE KINDS OF PEOPLE WHO CAME AND TRY TO DISRUPT ANYTHING. EVERYBODY JUST WENT THERE JUST TO BE. EVERYBODY JUST LIVED IT.

—Jeffrey Karasik

Quill

AUGUST 16, 1969

SET LIST

They Live the Life / That's How I Eat / Driftin' / Waitin' for You

QUILL WAS FOUNDED BY BROTHERS Jon and Dan Cole in 1967. The group, whose music was somewhat similar to early Alice Cooper, played the northeastern US circuit, hitting New York and New England many times over.

Dan Cole said that Michael Lang saw them perform in New York City and invited them to open day two at Woodstock. Day one had been dominated by the folkies, so Quill would have the privilege of plugging in and turning Woodstock into a rock festival.

He said that Lang also asked them to be musical goodwill ambassadors. The locals in Wallkill and beyond weren't particularly enthusiastic about having a massive music festival in their backyard, and if the group were to perform for free at local venues, maybe it would thaw relations a bit.

The local gigs, however, were not at clubs.

"There was one place, it was a prison for the criminally insane," Cole said. "They had us playing in the lunchroom."

When the band—who were behind cage screens—started playing, he said that the patients went "kind of semi-nuts," though he was not certain if it was because they liked the music.

"Who the hell knows?" he said. "Your guess is as good as mine."

The moment of truth finally came just after noon on that Saturday. Cole said that to the best of his recollection, the group was well received, even if the circumstances made it hard to tell.

"It's very hard to know exactly how people responded since you're outdoors, and half the crowd is a hundred yards or more away from you," he said. "It's not even like in an arena, or even a football stadium, where at least the noise is somewhat contained, so that you can gauge it. It's all going up in the air."

Still, he said that Quill had at least one very enthusiastic fan that day.

"During most of our performance, there was some guy who was totally naked, hanging out of the scaffold, jumping around in time to the music," he said.

In 1970, Quill released their debut album. It was also their last. The Woodstock appearance gave Quill's profile a bit of a boost, but it was temporary.

Cole said that the band petered out due to lack of promotion. They had been signed by Ahmet Ertegun, who had signed Led Zeppelin and Crosby, Stills & Nash, but when Quill didn't appear in either the *Woodstock* documentary or the soundtrack, Ertegun, incensed about the lost promotion opportunity, lost interest in Quill.

Boston's Quill opens day two of Woodstock. "I'm facing the camera," said singer and guitarist Dan Cole. "The person in the red shirt is guitarist Norm Rogers. You can see the sleeve of bassist Jon Cole's purplish T-shirt on the very left-hand side of the pic."

"The album was actually received relatively well by reviewers, but you have to get somebody pushing it," he said. "The music business is a very tough business, just like all the rest of the entertainment business."

To Cole, the event is firmly in the past, and while he could grouse about how it didn't lead to bigger and better things, he keeps things in perspective.

"If Quill had not been at Woodstock, we would have been a long-forgotten band that was once popular in the Boston and New York area and got to a certain place and disbanded," he said. "The only thing is, we had this sort of spike in our notoriety called 'Woodstock.'"

Cole added that he appreciates the opportunity for what it was, and he called it the right thing at the right time.

"Woodstock was fun," he said. "I was twenty years old, and what else would you want to be doing at twenty?" ◆

Country Joe McDonald

THE SECOND PERFORMER ON Saturday, August 16, was Country Joe McDonald. He has the distinction of being the only person to perform at Woodstock twice—first by himself and the second time with his band, Country Joe & the Fish.

Born in Washington, DC, and raised in southern California, his parents were card-carrying communists, whose commitment to the cause was so strong they named him after Soviet dictator Joseph Stalin. At seventeen years of age, he enlisted in the US Navy.

His time in the armed forces might come as a surprise to some, considering the antiwar sentiment of his most famous song, "The Fish Cheer / I-Feel-Like-I'm-Fixin'-to-Die Rag." However, in a 2017 interview with *The New York Times*, McDonald said that there was no contradiction between the song's sentiments and his own experience.

"I'm not a pacifist, I've never been a pacifist," he said. "I served three years and change, two in Japan, and it wasn't a bad experience, I didn't come out with antimilitary views. I was proud to be a veteran, the connection I had with the other soldiers, but I also understood the military dysfunction of capitalism combined with a large bureaucracy."

After leaving the military, McDonald ended up in Berkeley, California, after an unsuccessful attempt at earning a college diploma. While he was there, he recorded the songs "Who Am I?" and "I-Feel-Like-I'm-Fixin'-to-Die Rag," the latter of which he claimed to have written in just thirty minutes.

The connection that he said he had formed with other soldiers informed his approach to the song.

"I was inspired to write a folk song about how soldiers have no choice in the matter but to follow orders, but with the irreverence of rock 'n' roll," he told *The New York Times*. "It's essentially punk before punk existed."

Originally, he was only supposed to perform at Woodstock on Sunday with his group, but the scheduled second band of the day, Santana, was not ready to go on yet. McDonald was handed an acoustic guitar and asked to go up there and shake his moneymaker.

Country Joe McDonald teaches a crowd of over 400,000 people about the joys of spelling.

"I turned around and found Joe McDonald, who'd come just to listen to music because he's a musician, and he wanted to hear it," said John Morris. "He was up on stage, and I said, 'Joe, do you remember in Amsterdam, a few months ago, we talked about you wanting to try a solo career? Now!'"

McDonald agreed, but he didn't want to spoil the next day's set by performing any of the songs that he had scheduled. He performed a set that was mainly comprised of a bunch of old country-and-western songs, and when it was over, he decided to throw caution to the wind and play just one song from Sunday's set list.

"Give me an 'F!'" he yelled into the microphone.

The crowd roared back the letter "F."

They then followed his subsequent instructions to also shout back the letters "U," "C," and "K." Suddenly, the crowd was in the palm of his hand, and he performed "The Fish Cheer / I-Feel-Like-I'm-Fixin'-to-Die Rag." Those who couldn't be there to see it were afforded the opportunity to sing along with the lyrics by following the bouncing ball over the subtitles in the *Woodstock* documentary.

It was such a perfect moment that it's tempting to assume that it had been planned all along. But it was indeed a spontaneous decision, and like another spontaneous moment, Richie Havens's performance of "Freedom," it was one of the most memorable moments of the entire festival.

Its placement in both the documentary and the soundtrack pretty much cemented its place in history. Not bad, considering that according to the book *Noise: The Political Economy of Music* by Jacques Attali, McDonald was fined five hundred dollars and sentenced to having his head shaved when he uttered the dreaded "F" word at a performance in Massachusetts later in 1969.

The song also caused problems for McDonald in 2003 when he was sued for copyright infringement by Babette Ory, daughter of bandleader Kid Ory. She alleged that the "One, two, three, what are we fighting for?" portion of the song's chorus had been cribbed from the 1926 song "Muskrat Ramble," which had been cowritten by her father.

The case, *Ory v. Country Joe McDonald*, 68 U.S.P.Q.2d 1812 (C.D.Cal. 2003), ended with Ory not only losing, but having to reimburse McDonald for thousands of dollars' worth of attorney's fees, which she had to pay by selling her copyright to the song. Whoops.

McDonald left the stage, and he would be back the next day to perform with the Fish. ◆

Santana

SET LIST

Waiting / Evil Ways / You Just
Don't Care / Savor / Jingo /
Persuasion / Soul Sacrifice /
Fried Neckbones and Some Home Fries

SANTANA WAS WOODSTOCK'S TRUE breakout star. The overwhelming consensus on the part of the audience, the band, and the festival organizers was that this appearance turned them into a major act, overnight.

"They just burned the place down," said audience member Dan Sorenson, who was twenty. "They were so fucking good."

The band was formed in San Francisco in 1966 around guitarist Carlos Santana and singer and keyboard player Gregg Rolie. Their sound combined blues, rock, and Latin rhythms, an unprecedented combination at the time, and at first, nobody knew what to make of it.

The group spent its first years honing its sound in such Bay Area venues as the Fillmore West, but truly solidified with the addition of drummer Michael Shrieve. He provided a solid, rock counterpart to the Latin percussion that was already a major component of the group's sound.

Santana recorded its self-titled 1969 debut in May, and while Bay Area audiences were fans of their long-form, epic jams, Bill Graham, who was a strong advocate of the band after booking them at the Fillmore many times, had encouraged them to put shorter, more commercial songs on the album as well. One of them was "Evil Ways," their breakout hit.

Graham had been asked by the Woodstock promoters to lend some of his know-how to their effort, and he agreed, on the condition that the group was put on the bill. According to promoter Michael Lang, that was no problem so far as he was concerned.

"Bill sent me a tape of them and I fell in love with them," Lang said. "They hadn't recorded yet. They were a local band in San Francisco. I just loved what they were doing."

Santana's performance was one of the highlights of the festival, the movie, and the soundtrack album, and it made them stars instantly. This all happened while Carlos Santana was high on mescaline.

"When we first got there, around eleven in the morning, they told us we weren't going on until eight," he told *Rolling Stone* in 1989. "So I said, 'Hey, I think I'll take some psychedelics, and by the time I'm coming down, it'll be time to go onstage and I'll feel fine.' But when I was peaking around two o'clock, somebody said, 'If you don't go right now, you're not gonna go on.'"

The guitarist's state was referenced by none other than the forty-fourth president of the United States, Barack Obama, in his remarks at the 2013 Kennedy Center Honors reception at the White House, when Carlos Santana was inducted.

"When a twenty-two-year-old Carlos Santana took the stage at Woodstock, few people outside his hometown of San Francisco knew who he was," the president said. "And the feeling was mutual. Carlos was in such a—shall we say—altered state of mind that he remembers almost nothing about the other performers. He thought the neck of his guitar was an electric snake."

Be that as it may, the performance is remembered as one of the festival's high points, and the accolades were not limited just to the guitar-playing. The entire band earned raves.

"Michael Shrieve with Santana, I mean, his drumming was fierce, great drumming," said a fan identifying as L. Broido, who was eighteen. "I thought they were just unbelievably great."

The lineup that performed at Woodstock didn't last long. By the time the group's fourth studio album, *Caravanserai*, was released in 1972, original bassist David Brown and original percussionist Michael Carabello had left the group. Keyboard player Gregg Rolie, who had cofounded the group and sung their first hit, "Evil Ways," followed suit shortly thereafter, leaving to form the group Journey.

Santana the band has undergone countless lineup changes since then. More than seventy musicians have gone through its ranks, but don't interpret that as a sign that the band is in trouble. Carlos Santana is still going strong, over twenty studio albums later, and one of them, 1999's *Supernatural*, sold twelve million copies in the United States, according to *Billboard*—a smash hit by any metric.

Still, a lot of people have maintained that the lineup that performed at Woodstock was the group's finest, and those people were no doubt happy in 2016 when the group released *Santana IV*, which reunited most of the members of the Woodstock lineup. Carabello, Rolie, and Shrieve were all there, and Carlos Santana said that the bond between them had only strengthened over the years.

"We can now offer each other forty-five years of acquired wisdom," he told *Rolling Stone*. "We all have a deeper appreciation for one another, and now we have a second chance." ◆

John Sebastian

AUGUST 16, 1969

SET LIST

How Have You Been / Rainbows All
over Your Blues / I Had a Dream /
Darlin' Be Home Soon /
Younger Generation

JOHN SEBASTIAN'S SONGS ARE PART of the fabric of American music. He wrote "Do You Believe in Magic?" and "Summer in the City," songs that he recorded with his original group, the Lovin' Spoonful, and also "Welcome Back," the theme song to the 1970s sitcom *Welcome Back, Kotter*.

He founded the Lovin' Spoonful amid the folk music boom of New York City's Greenwich Village, and although it wasn't strictly a folk group, they were embraced within that scene anyway. Rock audiences, meanwhile, also embraced them.

The group was short-lived. Their debut album was released in 1965, and in 1968, Sebastian left to pursue a solo career. Both MGM and Reprise claimed the rights to the solo album that he recorded, and his career came to a halt while they battled it out.

With his career in a holding pattern, he went to Woodstock, intending to go just as a fan, not as a performer. The fact that he even got there was nothing short of a miracle.

He told the *Wall Street Journal* that producer Paul Rothchild had asked him if he wanted to go, and he agreed, but he couldn't get a flight to take him any closer than Albany, still a long way away.

At the airport, he saw his old road manager, Walter Gundy, loading a helicopter with the equipment that was going to be used later by the Incredible String Band.

"I had my ride," he told the *Wall Street Journal*. "Twenty minutes later, I was at the concert."

Although some sources say that Santana had already performed when he arrived, Sebastian remembered it differently. He told the *Wall Street Journal* that it had been raining, and when it stopped, the crew still needed time to get the rainwater offstage so that the next band—which Sebastian said was Santana—could turn on their amplifiers without getting shocked.

"Michael [Lang] turned to me and asked if I'd do it," Sebastian told the *Wall Street Journal*. "Tim Hardin loaned me his Harmony Sovereign guitar."

John Morris's recollection of how he became a performer at Woodstock differed from Sebastian's.

John Sebastian, who may or may not have been on LSD, performs an unplanned set for the crowd.

"Somebody said to me, 'John, John Sebastian is walking down the road, dressed from head to toe in tie-dye, carrying a guitar,' and I said, 'Don't waste time telling me, go get him'," Morris said. "They put him on. He was stoned, but it was wonderful, and he was a big help."

The set consisted of just five songs. He flubbed some of the lyrics, possibly because he had been shoved in front of over 400,000 people with no preparation. There was also the matter of the LSD that he may or may not have taken, according to the book *Woodstock: Three Days that Rocked the World*.

Despite that, the success of Sebastian's solo career was helped immensely by the performance, which put him back in the public eye.

"It was just one of those nice accidents, and it resulted in my career then taking another step forward," he told ClassicBands. com. ◆

The Keef Hartley Band

AUGUST 16, 1969

SET LIST

Spanish Fly / She's Gone / Too Much
Thinkin' / Believe in You / Rock
Me Baby / Sinnin' for You / Leaving
Trunk / Just to Cry / Sinnin' for
You (Reprise)

THE KEEF HARTLEY BAND WAS formed by British drummer Keith Hartley, who regularly performed in a Native American headdress and face paint. Before Woodstock, his most high-profile gig was as a member of John Mayall's Bluesbreakers, which he left at Mayall's urging to found his own group.

Mayall had sent Hartley packing with good intentions, and one need only listen to the opening of the Keef Hartley Band's debut, *Halfbreed*, to see that this was the case. It begins with a mock phone call of John Mayall "firing" Hartley.

The album got a warm reception from record buyers on both sides of the Atlantic, and the US tour that was organized to take advantage of it included a slot at Woodstock, according to the book, *Decca Studios and Klooks Kleek: West Hampstead's Musical Heritage Remembered*.

Hartley said in a 1994 interview in the *Lancashire Evening Post* that the group was booked not just because they were gaining notice in the States, but because of some practical concerns on the part of the organizers.

"They were hiring some incredible names, but they had a fixed budget to stick to, so they needed some lesser-known names as well," Hartley said. "I can't remember what we were paid now, but it was two or three thousand dollars, and I got the lion's share!"

The Keef Hartley Band was unable to parlay the festival appearance into greater commercial success. Lee Zimmerman of the *Broward Palm Beach New Times* attributed the group's lack of post-Woodstock superstardom to having to go on after Santana.

Hartley, meanwhile, blamed a poorly sequenced set list.

"We had our set list sorted and started with a slow number," he said. "It went downhill from there."

Michael Lang was a fan of the band, but he conceded that their appearance didn't do much for them.

"I liked the band a lot, just all of a sudden it didn't go anywhere," he said.

The group's greatest commercial success came with their 1970 album *The Time Is Near*. According to AllMusic.com, this was their only album to achieve chart placement in the United States and United Kingdom. The group's fortunes declined slowly but surely

after that, and after its fifth album, 1972's *Seventy-Second Brave*, the group disbanded.

Hartley released the solo album *Lancashire Hustler* in 1973, and was part of the group Dog Soldier, which released a single, self-titled album in 1975. After that, he scaled back his musical activities considerably, working only occasionally with John Mayall and with guitarist Michael Chapman.

For a while, he was completely divorced from the music business, running a carpentry company in the UK town of Preston, according to *Billboard*. He was said not to even own a drum kit anymore. But in 2003, he returned with the album *Not Foolish, Not Wise*, a full thirty years since the last Keef Hartley Band album was released. He died eight years later, at the age of sixty-seven. ◆

They were hiring some incredible names, but they had a fixed budget to stick to, so they needed some lesser-known names as well. I can't remember what we were paid now, but it was two or three thousand dollars, and I got the lion's share!

—KEEF HARTLEY

The Incredible String Band

AUGUST 16, 1969

SET LIST

Invocation / The Letter / Gather
Round / This Moment / Come with Me /
When You Find out Who You Are

THE INCREDIBLE STRING BAND WAS a group from Scotland, formed in 1965 by Mike Heron, Clive Palmer, and Robin Williamson.

Their music was categorized as folk, mostly because they played acoustic instruments, but their sound was more sophisticated and esoteric than anything that got lumped in with the label. And while nobody's accusing anyone of anything, a quick listen to some of Led Zeppelin's more Middle Eastern–tinged songs suggest that Jimmy Page may have listened to them a couple of times (wink wink).

The group was discovered by Joe Boyd, an American record producer who was opening a new extension of Elektra Records in Great Britain. Their self-titled debut was released in 1966, and it sounded like little else at the time.

Their fourth album, 1968's *Wee Tam and the Big Huge*, achieved chart placement in both the United States and the United Kingdom, and their increased profile led to them being offered a slot at Woodstock.

The band was scheduled to perform on Friday, the day that belonged to the folkies, but they didn't want to perform in the rain and asked to be pushed back to Saturday. It was an understandable choice, but they paid for it. When they took the stage, they were stylistically out of step with the rest of the day's performers.

"They are a great band, but they were not really the kind of band to be playing at that kind of a huge festival, with 400,000 people," said Canned Heat drummer Fito de la Parra, who watched their entire set. "It was very acoustic and very soft and mellow."

Canned Heat's manager, Skip Taylor, also saw the set.

"There was total quiet from the audience," Taylor said. "They were just completely inattentive, and the band was playing nothing that was inspiring or getting to them."

One person who was both attentive and inspired was Wavy Gravy. He said that he was too busy working to watch many of the performers, but he and his wife were fans and made a point of watching the group.

"We enjoyed the String Band," he said. "But mostly, I was working."

The Incredible String Band did not appear in the *Woodstock* documentary or on the soundtrack. Had they followed up the appearance with a popular album, it might not have mattered, but *Changing Horses*, released in November 1969, was not well received. Music journalist Robert Christgau characterized it as "the usual magic bullshit."

In 1997, Boyd wrote in the *Guardian* that prior to the recording of *Wee Tam and the Big Huge*, the group had gotten involved with the Church of Scientology. At first, it seemed like a positive step, because the band gave up drugs and alcohol and became much easier to communicate with. The quality of the music, on the other hand, took a hit.

"ISB's output lost its inventiveness, its charm, and the wild beauty of its melodies," he wrote. "They were more efficient in the studio, but there were fewer moments of surprise and inspiration."

The band also decided that they wanted to go on tour as a traveling pageant, called "*U*." It had dancers, sets, and a very high price tag. "Audiences began to level off,'" he wrote. "We lost a great deal of money."

The group released its last album, *Hard Rope & Silken Twine*, in 1974, and broke up. ◆

Canned Heat

AUGUST 16, 1969

CANNED HEAT WAS FORMED IN Los Angeles in 1965, and by 1969, they had become very familiar with the festival circuit. So familiar, in fact, that bassist Larry Taylor said he didn't think that Woodstock would be any different from any of the other festivals that they had already played.

"We did Monterey Pop," he said. "Then there was Miami, there was Atlanta, there was San Francisco, all these festivals during that era. So who knew we'd be talking about Woodstock fifty years later?"

Drummer Fito de la Parra said that the night before Woodstock, the band had played at the Fillmore East. They traveled from New York City to Bethel separately from their roadies, who hauled the equipment by truck. He said that it took the roadies twelve hours to get there, and they had to lift cars physically, by hand, to do it.

"They would get eight or ten people and they would move the cars aside, so the truck could go on and Canned Heat could go there and boogie," he said. "I call the roadies the infantry of rock and roll. There were very difficult circumstances, and they were there on time, delivering the equipment…we were one of the few bands that had all the equipment there."

The band, meanwhile, got there by commandeering a helicopter full of reporters at Wallkill Airport.

"[Singer] Bob Hite said to one of the reporters, 'Where do you think you're going?' And the reporter said, 'We're going to report the news'," said manager Skip Taylor. "Bob grabbed the guy and pulled him out of the helicopter, and said, 'We're going to *make* the news!'"

Jonathan Paley was a fourteen-year-old who got to see the performance.

"When Canned Heat was playing, somebody whipped this orange at Bob Hite," he said. "He caught the orange, then he put half the orange in his mouth, with the peel, and basically ripped it open and sucked out the juice. And I swear to God, if nobody else remembers this, he said, 'It tastes like pussy!' I swear to God he said that."

De la Parra said that he believed Canned Heat had one of the best receptions of anyone who performed at Woodstock, if not *the* best.

"It was just amazing," he said. "Overwhelming, you know, half a million people just going nuts."

Skip Taylor said that when the set was over, he saw a limousine parked backstage. The driver wasn't there, but the keys were in the ignition. They drove away but were soon thwarted by several parked cars, which Hite dealt with in a move perhaps inspired by the roadies.

"Bob Hite got out and rounded up seven or eight guys that were just walking around out there and started moving cars," Skip Taylor said. "Like, lifting their front over and then the back over."

The group found a Holiday Inn, and Skip Taylor went in and approached the front desk. The clerk wasn't there, but his guest list was, and it said that ten rooms were reserved for Big Brother and the Holding Company.

When the clerk returned, Skip Taylor identified the group as Big Brother and the Holding Company, and that night everyone in Canned Heat got to sleep at a hotel. The real Big Brother and the Holding Company never showed up.

The punchline to the limousine story was not revealed until many years later.

"I don't know, ten years later or something, we were in New York and we're driving in a limo from JFK Airport into the city," Skip Taylor said. "Somebody was telling this story, or parts of it, and all of a sudden the limo driver slams his brakes on and pulls to the side of the road and goes, 'You sons of bitches, that was my car!'"

Canned Heat was plagued by tragedy after Woodstock. In 1970, founding guitarist Alan Wilson died of a drug overdose, and Bob Hite died in 1981 after a performance. Fito de la Parra told *Ultimate Classic Rock* that

TOP: Canned Heat brings the boogie to the Catskill Mountains. (l-r) Guitarist Alan Wilson, singer Bob Hite, and bassist Larry Taylor. BOTTOM: Canned Heat drummer Fito de la Parra plays on his own drum kit instead of a borrowed one, thanks to the group's stalwart roadies.

the singer also died of a drug overdose, after ingesting heroin that was given to him at a show by a fan. But despite all the heartache and turnover, Canned Heat is still going strong and is still heavily identified with Woodstock.

"We are still here, and of course we are still known as a famous Woodstock band," de la Parra said. "'Going up the Country' is pretty much the theme of Woodstock." ◆

Mountain

AUGUST 16, 1969

SET LIST

Blood of the Sun / Stormy Monday /

Theme for an Imaginary Western /

Long Red / For Yasgur's Farm /

Beside the Sea / Waiting to Take You

Away / Dreams of Milk and Honey /

Guitar Solo / Blind Man / Dirty

Shoes Blues / Southbound Train

WHEN MOUNTAIN PERFORMED AT Woodstock on August 16, it was the fourth time they had ever played together in front of an audience.

The group was born when Cream producer Felix Pappalardi saw guitarist Leslie West perform with a group called the Vagrants and offered to produce a solo album for him. The 1969 album, *Mountain*, featured Pappalardi on bass, drummer N. D. Smart, and keyboard player Norman Landsberg.

Landsberg went his own way afterward, and Pappalardi replaced him with Steve Knight, a keyboard player who had been a member of several unsung bands, such as the Feenjon Group and Devil's Anvil. Now dubbed

Mountain, this was the lineup that played at Woodstock.

Zoe Knight, Steve Knight's daughter, said that the band members were not aware of the scale of the event at which they were about to perform. It didn't really sink in until they got there.

"He talked about how they didn't really understand what the festival was, and when they arrived, it was a huge surprise," she said.

She added that her father had said that he was alarmed by the conditions in which the attendees found themselves.

"He couldn't understand how any of the crowd could survive, considering the rudimentary conditions and just the sheer number of bodies there," she recalled.

During their set, Mountain performed songs from West's solo album and others that would appear on the group's 1970 album, *Climbing!* One was an as-yet-untitled song which would eventually be called "For Yasgur's Farm," in honor of the man who had made the weekend possible.

Not long after Mountain's hourlong, eleven-song set was in the history books, N. D. Smart parted ways with the group. However, unbeknownst to him, he had already made history, and not just for performing there.

Mountain had performed the song "Long Red" during their set, and the drumbeat from the Woodstock performance would go on to be sampled countless times decades later. It was sampled by Jay-Z for his song "99 Problems," and has been sampled so often by other artists that the Apple Music streaming service created an entire playlist consisting solely of songs in which Smart's performance appears.

Pappalardi died in 1983 when his wife, Gail Collins, shot him, under circumstances that remain unclear. According to *The New York Times*, she was charged with second-degree murder and criminal possession of a weapon and convicted of criminally negligent homicide.

She served two years in prison. After her release, she lived as a recluse in Mexico, where she died in 2014.

"She left instructions for her cats to be euthanized so their ashes could be mixed with hers," Joan Montgomery, a neighbor, told the *New York Daily News*. "Who does that?"

Mountain was resurrected in 1985, but Knight didn't participate. According to his daughter, he was always ambivalent about his experience at Woodstock.

"My dad was really happy to have been part of musical history, but he sometimes felt like the fame of it eclipsed his other musical endeavors," she said.

Knight, who had grown up in the town of Woodstock, served as a councilman for the town from 2000 to 2007, according to the *Hudson Valley One*. He died in 2013. ◆

Guitarist Leslie West of Mountain, whose Woodstock performance would be sampled by Jay-Z decades later.

Grateful Dead

AUGUST 16, 1969

SET LIST

St. Stephen / Mama Tried / Dark Star / High Time / Turn on Your Lovelight

*I*F ANYONE SHOULD HAVE PERFORMED brilliantly at Woodstock, it was the Grateful Dead. No band better personified the ethos of the hippie movement, and no band was better positioned to connect with thousands of people on acid.

In reality, there were huge struggles just to get them onstage, and once they got there, it wasn't worth it.

The band was the ninth to go onstage on Saturday. There had been delays due to rain and technical problems, and then the band caused problems of their own.

"We wanted them to play a longer set," said Joel Rosenman. "Their manager [Rock Scully] said, 'Not only are we not going to play a longer set, but the word is your check is not good, so we want cash or we're not going on.'"

Artie Kornfeld thought this violated everything the group represented, and he said so to Scully.

"Rock is a friend of mine," Kornfeld said. "I said 'Rock, Rock, if I just put this up, publicitywise, I could wipe out what the Dead stand

for. I can't believe that Jerry [Garcia] and Phil [Lesh] are telling me they can't go on.' And he said, 'Artie, but these guys want ranches and they want Land Rovers and they're always broke because they're playing for free all the time.'"

It would be nice to say that when the Grateful Dead finally went onstage, they pulled out all the stops and played a set for the ages—one that encapsulated the hopes and dreams of those who had journeyed for miles to be part of history. Unfortunately, nothing even close to that happened.

"The Dead played horribly," Wavy Gravy said.

"They were godawful," said audience member Dan Sorenson. "Oh my God, they were horrible."

"They were just totally fucked up," said L. Broido, an audience member who was eighteen. "Jerry Garcia kind of spoke about there being two coasts or one coast. He stood up there, obviously tripping, he said, 'Man this is crazy, what's with these people, this is like the West Coast, it's like the West Coast on the East Coast, it's like there's only one coast.'"

It wasn't just the audience members who had brutal criticisms of the group's set. No less an authority on the music of the Grateful Dead than singer, guitarist, and unofficial frontman Jerry Garcia felt the same way, according to *Ultimate Classic Rock*.

"Our set was terrible," he said. "We were all pretty smashed...On top of that, it was rain-

The Grateful Dead performing a set that almost everyone described as "terrible." That includes the band's own frontman, Jerry Garcia.

ing or wet, so that every time we touched our guitars, we'd get these electrical shocks."

Michael Lang said that Owsley Stanley, then the largest producer of LSD in the United States and also the group's sound man, was responsible for that particular aspect of the situation.

"Owsley decided to rewire their stage right before they went on, and so they were getting shocks and various other signals from their instruments," he said. "They had a really tough time."

Despite the problems that Lang described, he said that the group's performance was nowhere near as bad as many have said, including members of the group.

"That was the worst show they had ever played, they claimed," he said. "I didn't think it was as bad as they thought it was."

Ernie Brooks, who was in the audience, offered his own take on the set that differed wildly from all the one-star reviews.

"The Grateful Dead fulfilled every expectation," he said. "They were really good."

If the group's subpar set hurt their career,

you would never know it. They simply kept on recording and touring, and apart from releasing albums that consistently hit the *Billboard* Top 20 without mainstream radio airplay, they maintained the most rabid fan base on earth in the Deadheads, who dropped out of mainstream life to follow the band from tour date to tour date, all over the world.

In 1995, Jerry Garcia died of a heart attack. As the face of the band, the idea of them continuing without him seemed out of the question. But eventually, some of the surviving band members decided to keep going, doing so under different names, such as the Other Ones and the Dead.

In 2015, the remaining core members reunited for their *Fare Thee Well* tour. There were only five shows, so calling it a "tour" may be a bit of a stretch, but according to *Billboard*, the group was fifty-two million dollars richer when it was over. So while it may be too early to say, it looks like the Grateful Dead's lousy set at Woodstock did not have a negative effect on their career. ◆

Creedence Clearwater Revival

AUGUST 16, 1969

SET LIST

Born on the Bayou / Green River / Ninety-Nine and a Half (Won't Do) / Commotion / Bootleg / Bad Moon Rising / Proud Mary / I Put a Spell on You / The Night Time Is the Right Time / Keep on Chooglin' / Suzie Q

CREEDENCE CLEARWATER REVIVAL was one of the most popular bands of the 1960s. They hailed from the San Francisco Bay Area but stayed away from the region's trademark psychedelic jams. Instead, they focused on the three-minute single, and they were masters of the form.

"We grew up listening to Top 40 radio, and so the three-minute single, two-and-a-half-minute single, was the format," said bassist Stu Cook.

He said that when they reached the festival grounds in Bethel, they saw a lot of familiar faces. The experience that they had backstage bore no resemblance to the one that the audience was having.

"We hung out with Santana's people, the people from Bill Graham's organization took care of us," he said. "We hung out with him and drank wine and smoked weed, ate great steaks. Backstage was a different world and a half from the audience, for sure."

One thing that Bill Graham's organization could not provide was a reprieve from the hours of delays that plagued the entire festival. Cook said that the band endured a wait of several hours before they could finally set foot on stage.

"There was a lot of technical difficulties throughout the evening," he said. "We were supposed to play at ten on Saturday night, and I don't think we got on the stage until after one."

According to those who saw it, their set was a great one. Many audience members said it was one of the best performances of the weekend.

"Creedence was perfect," said Mark Yessin, who was twenty when he watched their set. "I thought the performance was great."

The band does not appear in the documentary or on the soundtrack. Cook said that

singer and guitarist John Fogerty refused to allow it on the grounds that the band had played too poorly. Cook was adamant that he was wrong about that.

"We had some technical problems at the start of the set," he said. "They were worked out, but I know John was irritated to no end about the problems that he was having, so maybe that caused him to have a different take on the evening. But we really did deliver that night. It was one of those not-ideal circumstances, but you try and rise to the occasion, and I believe we did."

When the set was over, the group left for their next concert. The contrast between that event and Woodstock could not have been clearer.

"We played the next day in a large circus tent with the Nitty Gritty Dirt Band somewhere in New Jersey," Cook said. "One night you're playing to half a million people, the next night you're playing to maybe five thousand or less. It was night and day for sure. It was like, 'Wow we just played for half a million people, and now we can count everybody here.'"

Three months later, the group released their fourth studio album, *Willy and the Poor Boys*, which was their third of 1969. Contemporary reviews called it their crowning achievement, but despite the accolades, the group only had three records left in them.

Guitarist Tom Fogerty, John Fogerty's older brother, left in 1970, and in 1972, they released *Mardi Gras*, their final album. The record was savaged by such critics as *Rolling Stone*'s Jon Landau, who called it, in a scathing review, "the worst album I have ever heard from a major rock band."

The group disbanded in October 1972, in a famously bitter breakup over such issues as management woes and personal problems among band members. Even the death of Tom Fogerty in 1990 couldn't make a dent in the acrimony, and when the group was inducted into the Rock and Roll Hall of Fame in 1993, John Fogerty refused to perform with them, according to *Ultimate Classic Rock*.

Despite the lingering bad feelings, Cook said that the music he made with the group will endure long after those details are forgotten.

"It's a very unhappy story, what started out as junior high school buddies playing in a rock and roll band, to the heights that we achieved for a period," he said. "But the music lives on, and it's definitely a good catalog. So at least we didn't screw that part up." ◆

Janis Joplin

AUGUST 16, 1969

*A*S A WOMAN IN THE ROCK AND roll boys' club, Janis Joplin enjoyed an assured place in history the moment that she stepped into the ring. But it wouldn't have amounted to much more than a footnote fifty years later if she couldn't sing, and Janis Joplin, quite frankly, could sing her ass off.

Her musical career took off when she joined the San Francisco band Big Brother and the Holding Company. They played at Monterey Pop, but she was the one who got all the attention—so much so that when Columbia Records reissued their self-titled debut in 1967, the cover was changed to add the words "featuring Janis Joplin" next to the group's name. If anyone needed confirmation that she would never be just another member of the band, this was it.

Joplin recorded one more Big Brother and the Holding Company album, 1968's *Cheap Thrills*, which featured "Piece of My Heart," one of her signature songs. She left shortly

thereafter and went solo, forming the Kozmic Blues Band to use as her backing group.

She had never been shy about her drug and alcohol consumption, but by the time of her Woodstock performance, she was regularly indulging to a degree that had grown more alarming to those who knew her. John Morris had hoped to help her by providing her with a place that was far enough from her usual haunts that she might be able to dry out a bit.

"I had a house in the Virgin Islands, because I was involved in a hotel building project down there," Morris said. "Myra Freedman, who was Janis's PR, had called me and said, 'Could Janis go down there before the festival?' because she needed a rest, and I said sure."

The singer took him up on his offer, but the moment he saw her afterward on the festival grounds, it was clear that the getaway had not had the desired effect.

"Janis went down there and I didn't see her until she arrived at Woodstock," he said. "She came out of the performer's den with a bottle of vodka in one hand and a bottle of Southern Comfort in the other, totally wasted. And I said, 'Hey honey, how did you like my house in St. Thomas?' and she said, 'It was great, just like everywhere else. I fucked a lot of strangers.'"

> *How are you out there? Are you okay? You're staying stoned and you got enough water and you got a place to sleep and everything?*
>
> **—JANIS JOPLIN**

Joplin went onstage at two o'clock on Sunday morning. She approached the microphone and checked in with the audience.

"How are you out there?" she asked. "Are you okay? You're staying stoned and you got enough water and you got a place to sleep and everything?"

After that, her set began.

"Janis Joplin was over-the-top, passionately good," said audience member Don Stark. "I guess I've read since then that she was on all sorts of alcohol and narcotics, but she put on a hell of a performance no matter what she was fueled by."

Mark Yessin, who was also in the audience, had seen her perform many times before, and he said that her performance lived up to his very high expectations.

"Janis was wonderful," he said. "She was tremendous. Janis was always tremendous."

John Morris disagreed completely.

"It was the worst performance I ever saw, and I saw her give tons and tons of performances," he said. "She was just totally wasted. When they added her to the director's cut of the film, they had to redo the sound. Larry Johnson, bless his wonderful soul, who worked with Neil Young and worked on the sound of *Woodstock*, pulled a rabbit out of a hat to make that sound acceptable."

If her set was in any way subpar, Michael Lang said that it was less a matter of her performance and more the effect of the band that was backing her.

"She was great, the band was not great," he said. "It was a new band and they hadn't worked in whatever they were going to work in musically well enough, and it had a wet-blanket effect on their set. *She* was great. I mean her voice was perfect and her performance was terrific. But the overall effect of the set was less than wonderful."

A few weeks after her performance, *I Got Dem Ol' Kozmic Blues Again Mama!* was released. It would be the last album released in her lifetime. She died of a heroin overdose on October 4, 1970, at the age of twenty-seven. Her final album, *Pearl*, was released in January 1971. ◆

An "over-the-top, passionately good" Janis Joplin.

Sly and the Family Stone

AUGUST 16, 1969

*I*F I HAD TO PICK ONE ACT THAT HAD the most dramatic musical set, it would be Sly," said Michael Lang. "He just took everybody with him on a trip to church."

If you couldn't be there to see it, just watch the documentary or listen to the soundtrack album. Both demonstrate that Sly and the Family Stone, led by singer and multi-instrumentalist Sly Stone, did exactly what Lang said.

When you see it or hear it, it's easy to see how it made people forget the rain, the mud, the exhaustion, and just dance.

But it almost didn't happen.

"Sly wouldn't go out of his dressing room to go on," said John Morris. "I went to the dressing room, knocked on the door, did a 'Bill Graham' on him, grabbed him by both his lapels, lifted him up in the air and said, 'You are going on the stage in two minutes, and you are going to perform the best set of your life. Do you understand me?' And he went, 'Yes sir.'"

Morris's moment of tough love may seem excessive, but it did the job.

"He went out and they played the best set of their life, and it was fabulous," he said.

Michael Lang explained what was causing Stone's state at the time.

"I knew Sly pretty well and he was having trouble with drugs," he said. "One of the things he would do is just sort of hang in his dressing room and snort coke."

Despite their bandleader's state, the group resolved to make their set unforgettable.

"We just looked at each other, grabbed each other's hands, and said, 'Let's just go do our thing and do it the best we can,'" drummer Greg Errico told *Ultimate Classic Rock*.

According to many who saw it, they succeeded, turning in a set of pure, sustained euphoria and joy. Both in the documentary and on the soundtrack album, the group's energy comes through with ease and stands out as one of the highest points of the entire weekend.

It's three-thirty on Sunday morning, and Sly and the Family Stone are taking the crowd "on a trip to church."

Almost immediately after Woodstock, the group shrewdly released a new single, "Hot Fun in the Summertime," which fell just one spot shy of the *Billboard* chart's peak. It remained on the charts into October, despite the absence of a summertime in which to have fun. After the *Woodstock* documentary was released theatrically, "I Want to Take You Higher" was reissued as a single, making its second appearance in the Top 40.

The Sly Stone who was capable of the kind of performance that he turned in at Woodstock disappeared in 1970, when he left his home in the Bay Area for Los Angeles. Stone's life took a dark turn then, and it never recovered.

"Enter firearms, coke, PCP, goons, paranoia, isolation, and a mean-spirited pet pit bull named Gun," said *Vanity Fair* journalist David Kamp.

On July 27, 1970, almost a full year after Sly and the Family Stone's triumphant Woodstock appearance, the band was booked to perform a free concert in Chicago's Grant Park. It was a goodwill gesture from the band, who had been no-shows at concerts in the Windy City on more than one occasion and were starting to gain a reputation for it.

According to the *Chicago Tribune*, a rumor began to circulate through the crowd that Sly and the Family Stone were going to cancel yet again. Someone threw an unidentified object at the stage, and the crowd, who had been waiting for hours in the sweltering heat, began to riot.

"Whether it was a rock or a heavy Ripple wine bottle that first crashed into the stage is unimportant," the *Chicago Tribune* reported. "That first object, the object that touched off a war, was quickly followed by others—rocks, bottles, pieces of benches that had been destroyed during the long wait for music."

The group's music changed radically on 1971's mischievously named *There's a Riot Goin' On*. Fans of their poppier music couldn't handle the change in direction, and neither could critics.

"Listening to it is like watching a junkie nodding, each breath measuring the slow descent of his head as he drops his comb for the tenth time in two minutes," wrote *Rolling Stone* critic Vince Aletti.

The group released two more albums, 1973's *Fresh* and 1974's *Small Talk*, and finally dissolved.

Sly Stone himself eventually fell on shockingly hard times. In 2011, the *New York Post* reported that the former superstar was broke and homeless, living in a camper van in the Crenshaw neighborhood of Los Angeles.

"His fortune stolen by a lethal combination of excess, substance abuse, and financial mismanagement....A retired couple makes sure he eats once a day, and Stone showers at their house," the *Post* said.

His situation appeared to improve in 2015, when a jury found that he was owed

> *Cynthia's role in music history isn't celebrated enough. Her and sister Rose weren't just pretty accessories there to "coo" and "shoo wop shoo bop" while the boys got the glory. Naw. They took names and kicked ass while you were dancing in the aisle.*
>
> —QUESTLOVE

five million dollars in songwriting royalties. Unfortunately, that same year, the *Los Angeles Times* reported that Stone couldn't collect the money, as he had already assigned the royalties to a production company in exchange for 50 percent ownership.

Any sort of full reunion of the band that performed at Woodstock became impossible in 2015, when trumpeter Cynthia Robinson passed away at the age of seventy-one from cancer.

"Cynthia's role in music history isn't celebrated enough," the multifaceted musician Questlove said in *The New York Times*. "Her and sister Rose weren't just pretty accessories there to 'coo' and 'shoo wop shoo bop' while the boys got the glory. Naw. They took names and kicked ass while you were dancing in the aisle." ◆

The Who

AUGUST 16, 1969

SET LIST

Heaven and Hell / I Can't Explain / It's a Boy / 1921 / Amazing Journey /

Sparks / Eyesight to the Blind (The Hawker) / Christmas / Acid Queen /

Pinball Wizard / Do You Think It's Alright? / Fiddle About / There's a Doctor /

Go to the Mirror / Smash the Mirror / I'm Free / Tommy's Holiday Camp /

We're Not Gonna Take It / See Me, Feel Me / Summertime Blues / Shakin'

All Over / My Generation / Naked Eye

"IF YOU ASKED ME FOR THE SINGLE greatest moment that I have ever had as a concertgoer, it was the Who performing *Tommy* while the sun came up," said audience member Don Stark, who was seventeen years old at the time.

The moment may have been a perfect one that seemed preordained, but the promoters had to go to chaotic lengths to make it happen. In fact, the group didn't want to play the festival at all and had to be talked into it.

Who guitarist Pete Townshend asked for fifteen thousand dollars for the performance, but there was only eleven thousand dollars in the budget to pay them. The group accepted, but not without including a little dig at John Morris. The original pressing of their 1970 *Live at Leeds* album came with a copy of their agreement to play at Woodstock in exchange for eleven thousand dollars.

"That was Peter's way of getting even with me," Morris said.

Artie Kornfeld said that he was extremely put off by the group's behavior (Townshend's in particular) on the day of their performance. The group refused to play unless they were paid their full fee, in cash, before going on, and the promoters simply didn't have that on hand. There were no banks open at night on a Saturday, either.

Kornfeld said that he told the guitarist that there might be a riot if the group didn't perform, but Townshend was unmoved. The group wanted cash. Period.

"John Wolf, who was their road manager, made us open up a bank at ten or eleven o'clock at night and get the bank manager,"

Who frontman Roger Daltrey sings for the crowd at sunrise. Cash only, please.

said John Morris. "John Roberts and Joel Rosenman talked the bank manager into it, open up and give us cash so we could pay them in cash before they went on. And they got paid eleven thousand dollars."

With their demands met, the Who took the stage at five o'clock in the morning, and today, fans attest to the transcendence of their set. But in the decades since, Townshend has had complicated and contradictory feelings about the festival.

"Woodstock could have been a beginning, not an end," Townshend said in the book *Play On! Power Pop Heroes: Volume One*. "There were nearly a million very good souls there, with the best intentions. What went wrong? I don't know. Maybe nothing. I didn't have a good time. It was just another gig to me—a particularly tough one."

If Townshend wasn't having a good time, he wasn't alone.

"They turned out to be the biggest pain in the ass of the weekend," Michael Lang said.

"Pete was miserable about being there, he wanted to be home, he wasn't into the whole hippie thing. He was just a grump the entire time he was there. And you know, in a sense, it was the most important show they had ever done. But on the day, he was a real pain in the ass."

The Who spent most of the decade after Woodstock producing albums that were artistic triumphs, such as *Who's Next* and *Quadrophenia*. The entire time, drummer Keith Moon was nursing a drug and alcohol problem that was only getting worse.

The problem was most apparent when the group performed in San Francisco in 1973. According to *Rolling Stone*, Moon consumed a combination of brandy and horse tranquilizers, rendering him unconscious. The group plucked nineteen-year-old drummer Scott Halpin from the audience to help them finish the set.

Ironically, Moon died from an overdose of Heminevrin, a drug that he had been pre-scribed to help him quit drinking.

The Who broke up in 1983 but reunited several times in the 1980s and 1990s. In the new millennium, they resumed touring, earning some of the best reviews of their career. In 2002, just as they were firing on all cylinders, bassist John Entwistle died from what the BBC said was a cocaine-induced heart attack.

With Townshend and singer Roger Daltrey the only surviving original members, the band has soldiered on. In 2017, they embarked on the *Tommy and More* tour, which saw them perform all of *Tommy*, in its entirety, all over again. ◆

Jefferson Airplane

AUGUST 16, 1969

SET LIST

The Other Side of This Life / Somebody
to Love / 3/5 of a Mile in 10 Seconds /
Won't You Try / Saturday Afternoon /
Eskimo Blue Day / Plastic Fantastic Lover /
Wooden Ships / Uncle Sam Blues / Volunteers /
The Ballad of You & Me & Pooneil /
Come Back Baby / White Rabbit /
The House at Pooneil Corners

MICHAEL LANG SAID THAT THE FIRST band that he booked to perform at Woodstock was Jefferson Airplane. With the exception of the Grateful Dead, it's hard to think of a band more closely identified with the San Francisco sound.

Their classic lineup did not materialize overnight. Their first album, 1966's *Jefferson Airplane Takes Off*, featured singer Marty Balin, guitarists Jorma Kaukonen and Paul Kantner, bassist Jack Casady, drummer Skip Spence, and singer Signe Anderson. Anderson had given birth to her first child and didn't think she could bring a newborn baby on the road with a rock band, so she stepped aside and was replaced by Grace Slick.

Skip Spence was replaced by Spencer Dryden, and the classic lineup of Jefferson Airplane was in place. They recorded 1967's *Surrealistic Pillow*, which featured "Somebody to Love" and "White Rabbit." Both songs became Top 10 hits, and *Surrealistic Pillow* remains their best-known album.

The band was scheduled to play a prime, headlining slot at the Woodstock festival on Saturday, but Paul Kantner told *Wales Online* that thanks to the hours of rain delays and other technical issues, it didn't work out that way, and Jefferson Airplane went onstage over nine hours late, in full daylight.

"We were due to be on stage at ten p.m. on the Saturday night, but we didn't actually get on until seven-thirty a.m. the following day," he said.

The many hours that passed may not have been good for Jefferson Airplane, but they were great for Sha Na Na, who were playing Sunday.

"There were a lot of musicians playing on Saturday night who were stranded and couldn't get out of the festival site, so there were a bunch of hotel rooms that were available even though there were other people [booked to be] staying there," said Sha Na Na's Elliott Cahn. "My girlfriend [Suzanne] and I stayed in Grace Slick and Paul Kantner's room, and Suzanne ended up trying on Grace Slick's dresses, which were all sort of silky and flimsy and gauzy."

While Cahn's girlfriend was wearing Slick's clothes, Slick herself waited with the rest of her band to perform. She described the experience to *Rolling Stone* in 2014, in terms that were not exactly glowing.

"Joni [Mitchell] wrote, 'We are stardust, we are golden' and all that shit," Slick said. "I love Joni, but I didn't have quite the same take on it…We were onstage all night. I don't remember going to the bathroom or wanting to. We were smoking dope and drinking wine and sitting around. It was a very large stage. Then ten o'clock came and they'd say, 'You're playing in an hour.' Then we played at something like seven in the morning. It was light. You don't play rock and roll at seven in the morning!"

When the band finally went onstage, Slick greeted the exhausted crowd.

"All right, friends, you have seen the heavy groups," she said. "Now you will see 'morning maniac music.'"

Jefferson Airplane played fourteen songs, including "Volunteers," which appeared on the soundtrack album. When they finished, many attendees took it as their cue to pack it in. Audience member JoAnn Devitt was one of them.

"I had had enough," she said. "A lot of people left at that time. It was a long wait for Jefferson Airplane and people thought that the show wasn't going to continue, just because it took so long and it was such a mess. It was all muddy, there wasn't any food, it wasn't fun at all."

Jefferson Airplane didn't last very long after Woodstock. Dryden parted ways with the group in 1970, and in 1971, Slick was badly injured in a car accident near the Golden Gate Bridge. Marty Balin left the same year.

Jefferson Airplane broke up in 1972. With the exception of Spencer Dryden, the band that performed at Woodstock reunited in 1989 and released a final, self-titled album.

In 2005, Dryden passed away, and in 2016, Paul Kantner died, literally on the same day that original singer Signe Anderson did. Although she missed out on almost all of Jefferson Airplane history, Balin wrote a heartfelt farewell to her, along with the other deceased members, on his Facebook page.

"One sweet lady has passed on," he wrote. "I imagine that she and Paul woke up in heaven and said 'Hey what are you doing here? Let's start a band' and… Spencer was there joining in." Balin passed away in 2018. ◆

Drugs

According to most accounts, the overwhelming majority of Woodstock attendees were high throughout the festival. This also went for the musicians, organizers, crew, and just about everyone else.

"I don't know if *everybody* was high, but there were certainly people offering whatever you wanted," said audience member Marla Argintar.

According to attendee Andy Paley, who was sixteen, you didn't have to ask for pot for someone to hand it to you. In fact, you didn't even have to be conscious.

"I woke up, leaning on this tree, and someone had put an ounce of pot into my pocket while I was asleep," he said.

"We had an ounce of pot and we had an ounce of hash," said Gail Hayssen, who was

fourteen. She said that at one point, she and her friends were close enough to the stage that she could actually share her bounty with at least one Woodstock promoter.

"We were at fourth-row center, so we were very, very close, and the promoters were on the stage," she said. "We rolled an entire doob of hash, so, it had a lot of weight to it, and I flung it through the air and he received it, the guy with the curly hair. I got a nice smile when I threw that to him. I just felt like, it was a good feeling to know that something that I brought went there."

She said that she did speed too, mostly so that she could stay awake to see all the performers.

"I had that the first day that we got there," she said. "I think the guys that I was with were taking these pills to stay awake and they said, 'Here, try this, Gail.'"

Reporter Ethel Romm wrote in the *Huffington Post* that there was mescaline, psilocybin, and STP being sold on tables in the woods surrounding the event, under a sign that read "DRUG STORE."

Jim Mesthene, who was sixteen, said that the authorities tolerated almost all of it. At one point, he and several people were smoking hash out of a hookah, when a state trooper came over to them. They exchanged hellos, and then they asked the trooper how he was doing.

"'I'm having a good time,' he said. 'This is the easiest job I ever had. Nothing for me to do here.'"

The trooper did, however, maintain professional decorum.

"We offered him a hit on the pipe and he said, 'I'm working, I can't do that.'"

The relative lack of busts for marijuana didn't necessarily mean that local authorities were okay with it. It was a simple matter of space.

> *You could probably count the people who weren't using something on one hand.*
>
> —CAROL CLAPP

"As far as I know, the narcotics guys are not arresting anybody for grass," a state police sergeant told *Rolling Stone*. "If we did, there wouldn't be space enough in Sullivan County, or the next three counties, to put them in."

Woodstock attendees were widely reported to be polite and subdued, almost certainly thanks to the effects of marijuana. This was not lost on the authorities, nor was it lost on them how things could have turned out if pot hadn't been the drug of choice that weekend.

"If this crowd was drinking beer, they'd be violent," authorities told Ethel Romm. "This pot stuff quiets down everyone. There's thousands here. We couldn't have handled it." ◆

News Coverage

Woodstock caught almost the entire main-stream news apparatus of the United States off guard. *Rolling Stone* sent a team of journalists to cover it, but at the time, it was the counterculture's publication of record. Most of the country's major news organizations, on the other hand, missed the boat entirely.

Of the mainstream outlets that did cover it, many spent a lot of ink simply explaining basic hippie jargon. "Bethel Pilgrims Smoke 'Grass' and Some Take LSD to 'Groove',", was the headline of an article that ran in *The New York Times* on August 18, 1969.

"'Grass' is marijuana, and getting 'stoned' is getting high on it," Barnard Collier wrote. Forty years later, he explained that he had had to fight his editors for permission to cover the event at all. They didn't understand what it was, or why anyone might care.

"Now, everyone knows that stuff," he said. "Back then, nobody knew."

His editors relented, and he went to cover Woodstock. When he arrived, he realized that it wasn't only *The New York Times* that didn't understand what was going on. He walked into the press area that the promoters had set up, and it was empty.

New York Daily News reporter Jack Deacy covered the event from the ground. He arrived on the Wednesday before and stayed all the way through. He had received a press release from the promoters and figured that this was going to be big. When he got there and saw the grounds, he wasn't certain whether it could be pulled off.

"These people were not prepared in any way for this amount of people," he said. "The stage wasn't even built. When the rains fell, a lot of people were very uncomfortable. It was like a boot camp."

Deacy's piece didn't run until after the festival. Meanwhile, the *Times Herald-Record*, a local newspaper out of Middletown, New York, was one of the only publications to report from the scene in real time. Woodstock had been an ongoing source of local controversy when the promoters were

Wednesday, August 27, 1969 THE TIMES HERALD **RECORD**

4

Expo backers say $1 million covers debts

By GIL WEISINGER   NEW YORK

Woodstock Ventures, the youthful corporation that produced the Aquarian Exposition, has resorted to family and establishment to extract it from its financial bind.

Joel Rosenman, 26-year-old attorney and partner in the corporation, confirmed reports Tuesday that the family of Woodstock President John Roberts has agreed to stand behind the $1 million in still-outstanding debts.

Effective immediately, Rosenman said, all outstanding checks will be honored and be paid with cash supplied by the Roberts family, which made a fortune from Poli-Dent and other products of the Block Drug Co.

Woodstock intends to repay the family, Rosenman said. He added that the Roberts family has made "financial arrangements" with a New York bank to pay the Woodstock debts, although the $1 million has not been deposited.

While Rosenman declined to reveal the bank, a reliable financial source identified it as the National Bank of North America in New York.

The money was put up to handle the post-festival expenses incurred by the three-day festival which brought an estimated 500,000 people into Bethel the weekend of Aug. 15-17. Among the anticipated expenditures are claims by area residents seeking financial redress for damages allegedly caused to their property by the swarming hordes of youths.

Meanwhile Bethel taxpayers have called a public meeting at 7:30 p.m. Friday at the Presbyterian Church. One purpose of the session is to determine what legal recourse is open to gain compensation for claims.

Other purposes, according to a spokesman, are to discuss measures to prohibit another festival, and to "demand public answers" for alleged zoning violations and misconduct of some local officials.

Woodstock is reportedly following a parralel course by preparing payments. Rosenman, from his office here, said Tuesday that payments will be made this week. However, he was apparently unaware of the Friday meeting which could bring legal action.

"Everyone," Rosenman said, "has been remarkably patient and we are confident we will make good on our obligations." He pledged the promoters will "stay in the Bethel area until all obligations are consummated."

Of the substantial deposit allegedly made by Roberts, Rosenman commented, "We are speechless at the way Roberts's family rushed forward (with the money)."

Rosenman, 26, a lawyer who has been associated with Roberts, 24, in Woodstock Ventures, Inc., for two and a half years, will seek to recoup the $1 million through the sale of films and recordings made at the festival.

The promoters claim a ticket sale of 60,000 to 70,000 for each of the three days, with tickets costing $6.50. Listing all "possible" sources of income from the festival, Rosenman also included the motion picture and recording contracts ("for which we still have received no money"), revenue from books written on the mammoth event, sale of posters and emblems, and future promotions.

On the negative side of the financial picture, Rosenman said expenses will run "between $2 million and $3 million, representing a loss of more than $1 million."

While Rosenman could not determine the expense totals, he remarked "Wednesday (today) we will gather statistical information and have a more accurate picture."

The major debts still to be paid, he said, include payments for helicopters, medical supplies, and doctors.

He also named the sheriff's department as another expenditure and said, "We are working out something with the sheriff." Other major expenses included those for contractors, employees, and clean-up workers. About 70 clean-up employees, he added, are still working.

On the future of Woodstock, Rosenman was optimistic. The company will, he said, conduct another festival but it will be based on the "lessons learned" from the Bethel expo. "We must gear ourselves for numbers (of patrons) that, prior to the festival, were considered impossible.

"We felt that we overestimated the amount that would attend and we provided for the over-estimate."

The promoters, he said, were overwhelmed by the amount of patrons that appeared.

Rosenman said it would be premature to say whether the next festival would be in Bethel.

One area resident who said he would make a claim for damages was Ben Leon, a Bethel bungalow colony owner who rented two boats to Woodstock to use as a safeguard for swimmers.

He said he was paid $100 for the use of the boats, but when he attempted to deposit the check, it bounced several times. Beside the dispute over the compensation for the boats, he is also concerned over alleged damage incurred at the colony.

His claims against the promoters, totaling about $2,000, include an alleged loss of several mattresses when some youths broke into his bungalows.

--TH-Record photo by Gil Weisinger

Joel Rosenman, vice president of Woodstock Ventures, Inc., handles the job of coordinating Aquarian Exposition debts with resources while at his White Lake office.

Minister sees God's hand in Aquarian

TH-Record close-up

Aquarian Exposition: Messy, not violent

By DENIS M. THOET

Perhaps the most amazing but understated fact of the Aquarian phenomenon has been the transformation of a disaster - potent situation into what may best be described as a victory for the human spirit.

Politically activist groups, who had hoped to use the mass audience as forum, mobilized themselves and virtually saved the day in the dark hours when the entire operation was in danger of inundation and total collapse.

Private groups in the county, which at one time were verging on washing their hands of the entire event, pitched in to relieve the desperate food and medical

WHITE LAKE

The crowd itself never permitted bitterness to overcome despite the hardships of getting in, being rained on, confused, lost, and sick. Volunteers manned first-aid stations and hospitals as attendants and stretcher bearers, and campers near the Hog Farm took over food distribution in the free kitchens.

Stanley Goldstein, assistant producer of what he called "the largest gathering ever," spoke with tremendous admiration for all who participated. Goldstein was interviewed in his tent on the Hog Farm where he managed to grab three hours of sleep in the past two days.

"We've got the greatest staff in the world," Goldstein said. "The kids themselves proved that when given the opportunity they can do the job. They didn't have the tools but they coped beautifully.

The potentially dangerous situations Friday and Saturday occurred at the concession area, but were smoothed over almost immediately by members of the Hog Farm.

On Friday, six members of an ad hoc "free food" group raided the S and W ice cream station and liberated thousands of ice cream bars. On Saturday an undetermined number of a sabotage-oriented group from New York, whose name is unprintable, tore down two concession stands and made off with an undetermined amount of food. Both groups were protesting the sale of food, claiming it should be distributed free.

Other plans for political activism that may have ballooned into violence were transformed into a saving effort that transcended political and anti-establishment motivations.

"These people provided the major portion of the medical facility and staff during the critical rainy first night," Goldstein said. "Without detracting from the greatly appreciated efforts to airlift supplies through the army's and other efforts, the Medical Committee for Human Rights (was) the initial organizer of the airlift of 14 doctors from the city that arrived first to take a serious medical situation in hand."

Jeff Sarno, publisher of "Rat," a New York underground newspaper, used his portable press for producing newssheets and survival information to the burgeoning population. Goldstein said.

"Resist Communication," also of New York, established a mobile communications unit during the crisis and is credited with preventing a heavily taxed communications system from breaking down completely, according to Goldstein.

Beyond this the yippies, led by Abbie Hoffman, and the Students for a Democratic Society and other radical and anti-war groups swelled the Aquarian staff from 250 to 500.

Though this city has passed the original crisis and was about to recreate the biggest traffic jam in the history of the area, a certain calm and orderly chaos prevailed Sunday afternoon.

"It is pretty difficult for someone not to realize that we are in the midst of what can best be described as a disaster area, Goldstein said. "Still the crowd has succeeded in enjoying the music and each other. The hardships, in a way, have added a certain warmth to what is perhaps the greatest gathering ever."

THE TIMES HERALD RECORD   Wednesday, August 20, 1969   5

Ticket refunds out

Expo owners regroup, vow to pay off debts

By CHARLIE CRIST

WHITE LAKE

Owners of Woodstock Ventures, Inc., promoter of the three-day Aquarian Exposition, are refinancing and re-organizing accounts, and all checks will be made good Thursday.

This was reported late Tuesday by Mel Lawrence, executive director of the festival that closed early Monday morning amid divided opinions as to its success or failure.

Lawrence made the response to questions from The Times Herald-Record after it was reported that the branch office of the Sullivan County National Bank at White Lake had refused to honor a $100 Woodstock Ventures check presented by Ben Leon, a property owner in the Bethel site area.

Charles Prince, branch bank manager, referred The Times Herald-Record reporter to the main office at Liberty. However officials there were reported in conference and unavailable until today.

Questioned on where the money was coming from and if one of the Woodstock Ventures owners was connected in any manner with Ipana Toothpaste Co, Lawrence replied: "The money is coming from John Roberts's private fortune."

Roberts is the president of Woodstock Ventures Inc. Lawrence said there was no connection with Ipana. He also scoffed at reports of a firm broke or filing bankruptcy, but estimated losses of $1.5 million.

"It would be foolish to even consider it (bankruptcy)," he asserted "We have a commodity that can't be bought."

Lawrence was apparently referring to the "peace and love" advertised before the festival and the same "peace and love" that permeated the attitudes of the reported 500,000 young people who attended.

Woodstock will not refund ticket money, according to Lawrence. No tickets were collected at the site as the crowd, 10 times the 50,000 estimated earlier, swarmed over the fences.

Meanwhile Lawrence is charged with directing the massive clean-up of garbage and debris on and around the site.

Gradually the area is beginning to assume an atmosphere of normalcy. State Department of Public Works crews are clearing away the debris along Rt. 17B, which Monday resembled a 10-mile-long dump.

Lawrence's crews are burning rubbish but millions of empty beer and soda cans are being compacted and carried off to the Town of Bethel dump.

He estimated there were 150,000 yards of garbage to be cleared away and it is impossible to convert that into tonnage. He also disclosed that the State Board of Health has been advised of the effort and that it "understands the problem."

Two bulldozers and two tractors with rakes are working on the area, plus 20 employes and many volunteers.

An additional crew is surveying the area to determine damage to neighborhood fences and property to facilitate settlement and repairs.

Lawrence estimated that about 200-300 festival goers remained on the site and most of them were preparing to leave. Near Bethel and Monticello, few of the long-haired, hippie types were to be found Tuesday.

The garbage being plowed into a pile is only a tiny fraction of the 150,000 cubic yards of trash said to litter the 600-acre Aquarian Exposition site. Sign below, posted in front of Richard Joyner's general store on Rt. 17B, expresses one anonymous resident's feelings. --TH-Record photos by Charlie Crist

What ESTABLISHMENT is responsible for THE MESS you're leaving behind?

---

looking for a site, and covering it made sense for an area publication.

Ethel Romm and her husband, Al Romm, the newspaper's editor, did the reporting, only because no other reporter from the *Times Herald-Record* was able to get to the festival site at all because of the traffic. The Romms were only there because they had taken back roads.

The *Times Herald-Record* was able to report from the festival site because Al Romm, who passed away in 1999, had hired a courier to bring film and copy back to the newsroom on a motorcycle, which was the only way to get through the miles and miles of abandoned cars.

Dan Sorenson, who was twenty, had a portable radio with him and listened to the news coverage that came from people who couldn't reach the site. Most of the reports bore no resemblance to reality.

"It sounded like the end of the world," he said. "They made it sound like it was a death camp or something."

Years later, Sorenson worked in news, and he said the experience clarified for him why the coverage of Woodstock had been so negative.

"I understand the instinct to play up the drama," he said. "Nobody wants to hear, you know, 'Everything's fine here.'" ◆

Technical Difficulties

Woodstock was beset by technical problems before it even started, and those problems didn't stop until it was over. Some were more serious than others, and some were easier to address than others.

The stage was designed by production stage manager Steve Cohen, and its construction was supervised by lighting designer Chip Monck. Unfortunately, after the venue was moved from Wallkill, there simply wasn't enough time to get it done right.

The stage was designed as a turntable, so that one act could set up while another performed. Then the stage could be turned like a lazy Susan, cutting down on change-over time.

Chris Langhart said that the turntable stopped working after the first day. Joshua White of the Joshua Light Show remembered it differently, saying that it stopped working after going around exactly once, at which time the wheels broke off.

Either way, it was a problem, and it wasn't the only one that the stage had.

"It rained a lot and that was farm country, so the stage began to sink a little bit," White said. "Not to the degree that it was tilting. You know, it wasn't the *Titanic*. But it was a very unstable situation."

There were other problems as well, some that are clearly evident to anyone who watches the *Woodstock* documentary.

"If you look at the film, and you see me on the stage when the storm came up, I had a live mic shorting in my hand," said John Morris. "The towers were weaving back and forth, and the overhead trusses were weaving back and forth, and the wind was blowing over fifty miles an hour. So yeah, we had a couple of problems."

There were also issues that could have threatened the lives of the festival audience.

Joel Rosenman said that at one point, the chief electrician told him the cables that had been buried in the ground were becoming slowly unearthed. These cables carried thirty thousand volts of electricity to the stage.

"We experienced so much foot traffic that the cables are now unearthed, and now the kids are walking on the actual cables, and wearing away the insulation," Rosenman said. "Tens of thousands of wet hippies in bare feet are going to be standing on the very problem."

The chief electrician told Rosenman that

the only way to deal with it was to shut down the stage.

"I had no idea what that would disintegrate into," he said. "Just having these kids with nothing to do except complain about how bad it was, because it's sitting in mud, it was a huge line to get a hamburger and it was an hour and a half to go to the bathroom. The thought of pulling the plug on all this was horrifying to me."

The chief electrician said that it might be possible to bypass the exposed cables and use ones that were still buried and protected, but it would take at least half an hour. Rosenman told him to do it. He did, and the crisis was averted.

"That was a long half-hour," Rosenman said. ◆

I DON'T THINK WE SMOKED ANY DOPE THROUGH THE WHOLE THING AND I DIDN'T NEED IT. THE MUSIC DID IT. THE MUSIC WAS WONDERFUL. THAT WAS ALL THE HIGH WE NEEDED. THE WHOLE MINDSET WAS PEACEFUL. EVERYONE WAS HAPPY. JUST ENJOYING IT. AND A LOT OF PEOPLE THERE, I THINK, AND WE CAN TALK ABOUT THAT LATER, I THINK CARRIED THAT MINDSET ON THROUGH THE YEARS.

—Marla Argintar

THERE WAS NO DIFFERENCE BETWEEN WHERE THE AUDIENCE WAS AND WHERE THE ARTISTS WERE. THE FENCES BROKE DOWN, EVERYONE WAS EVERYWHERE. THERE WAS AUDIENCE BACKSTAGE. THERE WERE MUSICIANS OUT IN THE CROWD. THE LINE BETWEEN THE STAGE AND THE AUDIENCE WAS PRETTY MUCH GONE.

—David Clayton-Thomas, Blood, Sweat, & Tears

I STARTED HITCHHIKING. I GOT PICKED UP BY THIS BEAUTIFUL WOMAN IN A BRAND NEW 1969 CAMARO CONVERTIBLE. I WAS FOURTEEN YEARS OLD AND THIS WOMAN WAS PROBABLY ABOUT THIRTY, MAYBE LATE TWENTIES, BEAUTIFUL WOMAN. SHE SAYS, "WHERE ARE YOU GOING?" I'M JUST GOING UP THE ROAD HERE. AND SHE SAID, "WELL I'M GOING TO MONTREAL. YOU WANNA COME WITH ME?" I THOUGHT ABOUT IT FOR A SECOND AND I SAID NO. BUT I'VE ALWAYS WONDERED WHAT THE HELL SHE HAD IN MIND. ALL THESE YEARS I'VE WONDERED ABOUT THAT. WHAT WOULD'VE HAPPENED IF I SAID, "YEAH, I'LL GO TO MONTREAL."

—Jonathan Paley

Day Three Playlist

Listen to the artists who performed at Woodstock
on August 17, 1969, in the order in which they played.

WoodstockDayThreeSampler.com

Joe Cocker

AUGUST 17, 1969

WOODSTOCK'S THIRD AND FINAL day began at two o'clock in the afternoon with a performance by Joe Cocker. Artie Kornfeld said that he was instrumental in getting him added to the bill.

The British singer had recorded a radically reworked cover of the Beatles' "With a Little Help from My Friends," which turned the pleasant, shuffling original into a lumbering, swinging beast. Many artists have covered Beatles songs before and since, but few have ever made one truly their own in the way that Cocker did.

Kornfeld was already familiar with the singer, but when Michael Lang had initially chosen not to book him, Kornfeld hadn't pressed the issue.

That all changed when Kornfeld went to the Bahamas on vacation and found himself surrounded at his hotel's dice table by Island Records founder Chris Blackwell and record producer Denny Cordell. They had flown over from England to see to it that Cocker was booked at the festival.

"They tracked me down," Kornfeld said. "They flew from England to meet me at the Bahamas to talk to me privately about Cocker and Woodstock."

After that, he called Lang and insisted that Cocker be added to the bill.

"I'm telling you this guy is a smash," Kornfeld told Lang over the phone. "He's got to be in."

Lang agreed, and that was that.

Cocker was twenty-five years old when he performed at Woodstock, and while he had played more than his fair share of British clubs, he had never played to a crowd remotely close to 400,000 people in his life. According to *Ultimate Classic Rock*, he said that this "sea

A "sea of humanity" has its first contact with an obscure singer named Joe Cocker.

of humanity" was so huge that it was almost impossible to tell if they even liked him.

"It took about half the set just to get through to everybody, to that kind of consciousness," he said. "We did 'Let's Go Get Stoned' by Ray Charles, which kind of turned everybody around a bit, and we came off looking pretty good that day."

In addition to the music, the set included some unintentional slapstick comedy, courtesy of the stage crew. The Joshua Light Show's screen was being used as a makeshift rain canopy over the stage, and it had become loaded with rainwater thanks to the constant downpours.

"This tarp, or piece of canvas, became a water basket," Chip Monck said. "There was

a great deal of weight in that, and it had to be relieved."

Rather than carefully cover all the equipment onstage and push the screen up from the center, letting water spill out on all four sides, a crew member attached a knife to a bamboo pole and stabbed the screen in the center. It worked, but at the Sheffield singer's expense.

"During Joe Cocker's set, it emptied all of it on him," Monck said, adding that the singer didn't mind. "Joe was impenetrable. Nothing seemed to bother him."

Cocker ended the set with his famous Beatles cover, and he left the stage a star.

"An amazing performance," Michael Lang said. "Nobody had really known who he was."

After he finished, the rain became too strong for the performances to continue. Woodstock ground to a halt for several hours.

Cocker's performance appeared in both the documentary and on the soundtrack album, and it transformed him from popular singer to icon. This was never more evident

than when he performed on *Saturday Night Live* and cast member John Belushi joined him onstage, dressed as him, and did his impression of the singer at his side, writhing and undulating in the manner which Cocker had himself pioneered.

> *It took about half the set just to get through to everybody, to that kind of consciousness.*
> —JOE COCKER

In 1976, Woodstock came back into Cocker's life when Michael Lang agreed to manage him. The singer had entered a midcareer slump, and Lang managed to guide him back into the spotlight slowly over the next couple of years.

In 1982, he had the biggest hit of his career with "Up Where We Belong," a duet with Jennifer Warnes that was on the soundtrack to the movie *An Officer and a Gentleman*. He remained a steady live attraction afterward, touring consistently and recording. His final live performance was in 2013, and one year later, he passed away from lung cancer at age seventy.

According to the *Guardian*, his passing did not go unnoticed by the Beatles' camp.

"Goodbye and God bless to Joe Cocker from one of his friends, peace and love. R.," said Ringo Starr on Twitter. ◆

Country Joe & the Fish

AUGUST 17, 1969

SET LIST

Rock & Soul Music / (Thing Called) Love / Not So Sweet Martha Lorraine /

Sing, Sing, Sing / Summer Dresses / Friend, Lover, Woman, Wife /

Silver and Gold / Maria / The Love Machine / Ever Since You Told Me That

You Love Me (I'm a Nut) / Short Jam (instrumental) / Crystal Blues /

Rock & Soul Music (Reprise) / The Fish Cheer / I-Feel-Like-I'm-Fixin'-to-Die Rag

COUNTRY JOE MCDONALD HAD already performed at Woodstock on Saturday, but he still had his scheduled gig with the rest of his band to play. That took place on Sunday, several hours after Joe Cocker's appearance, which had been followed by pounding rain.

The group had its genesis when McDonald and Barry "The Fish" Melton met in the Bay Area and began performing together as a duo. The group's number expanded to six, and while they were first augmented by such instruments as the kazoo and the washboard, they went electric after McDonald was given LSD.

"We turned Joe on to acid," Melton said in the book *Eight Miles High: Folk-Rock's Flight from Haight-Ashbury to Woodstock*, by Richie Unterberger. "He needed it, or so we thought."

Melton said that after plugging in, the band quickly went from playing a couple of times a month to two shows a night. They soon went into the recording studio and made an EP, which contained the instrumental "Section 43." The song was an exotic slice of melancholic psychedelia that proved the group could do more than just spell "fuck."

The debut LP, *Electric Music for the Mind and Body*, was released in May 1967, and the second album, *I-Feel-Like-I'm-Fixin'-to-Die*, followed just six months later. The first cut, "The Fish Cheer/I-Feel-Like-I'm-Fixin'-to-Die Rag," was unusual for its time, in that it was clearly an antiwar song, but it was also really funny—all at a time when popular musicians didn't really "do" irony.

McDonald said on his own website that the song earned them a lifetime ban from

On Sunday, Country Joe McDonald came back to the Woodstock stage for his triumphant return engagement, one day after his impromptu solo set.

the Schaefer Beer Festival. *The Ed Sullivan Show*, which had paid them in advance for an upcoming appearance, let them keep the money, provided they stay away.

The group released *Together* in 1968 but soon started to suffer instability in its lineup. They released *Here We Are Again*, their most overtly pop album yet, in July 1969. One month later, they appeared at Woodstock, with an energetic performance that gave the weather a middle-finger salute and got the crowd moving.

"One Country Joe and the Fish partisan attached himself to their onstage exuberance and undulated into a psychedelic hula," Jan Hodenfield wrote in *Rolling Stone*. "Without missing a beat, he slipped out of all his clothes and, before an audience stretching into soggy infinity, wove his own melody of joy. Within the audience, another two young men, one black and one white, shed their uptightness with their clothes and, cocks jiggling, choreographed their own rain dance."

After 1970's *CJ Fish*, McDonald went solo. Anyone who thinks that he did so because his Saturday set had made him drunk with power should think again. McDonald said on his website that he never had even wanted to do it in the first place.

"There were too many people," he said. "I was scared. They found a guitar, a Yamaha FG 150, and tied a rope on it…and pushed me on stage. The rest is history." ◆

Ten Years After

AUGUST 17, 1969

TEN YEARS AFTER WAS LED BY guitarist Alvin Lee, who played a signature Gibson ES-335. He never became as famous as fellow guitar-slinging Englishmen Eric Clapton or Jeff Beck, but it certainly wasn't because he wasn't good enough. Just watch him perform the first ten seconds of "I'm Going Home" in the *Woodstock* documentary, and you can't escape the conclusion that he could really play.

Lee has said that as a child, he had been encouraged to play the clarinet by his family. Then he heard Big Bill Broonzy in his parents' record collection and moved over to the guitar. The clarinet never stood a chance after that.

He formed Ten Years After in 1967, and while their self-titled album didn't do much for them commercially, their next, the live *Undead*, was a whole different story.

It contained only five songs, the first of which, "I May Be Wrong, but I Won't Be Wrong Always," lasted for almost ten minutes. This showcased Ten Years After in their strongest context, the extended live rave-up, and the record-buying public responded.

Ten Years After's next couple of albums saw them expand their sound somewhat, but they wisely stuck to fleet-fingered guitar jams when they performed. Woodstock was no exception.

They kicked off their set at eight-fifteen in the evening with the blues standard "Spoonful," but the song that really lit the place up was "I'm Going Home," which they used to close their set. It had closed their *Undead* album too, but the Woodstock version easily outshines that one and should be considered the definitive take.

"They did a great set," Michael Lang said. "It was just great musicianship."

L. Broido, who described himself as "not a huge fan" of the group, was impressed nonetheless.

"Musically, at the time I was blown away by Ten Years After," he said. "I think they had an incredible set."

Alvin Lee distinguished himself as an excellent guitar player, during a weekend full of great guitar players. The performance

was included in the *Woodstock* documentary and on the soundtrack album, increasing the group's profile in the United States. Lee said that he found it amusing that they were emissaries of the blues in the country that had invented it.

"The strange thing was, we had gone to what I considered to be the home of the blues, but they'd never heard of most of them, and I couldn't believe it—'Big Bill who?'" he said in 2003, according to *The New York Times*. "We were recycling American music and they were calling it the English sound."

Ten Years After switched labels in 1971, leaving the Decca subsidiary Deram for Columbia. They released *A Space in Time*, which featured "I'd Love to Change the World," their biggest hit.

The band broke up in 1974. They reunited during the 1980s and 1990s, but in 2001, Alvin Lee was asked to take part in another reunion, and declined, according to AllMusic.com. He spent the rest of his career recording and performing under his own name, but his Woodstock performance remains the defining moment of his career.

He passed away in 2013 at the age of sixty-eight. ◆

> *The strange thing was, we had gone to what I considered to be the home of the blues, but they'd never heard of most of them, and I couldn't believe it— "Big Bill who?" We were recycling American music and they were calling it the English sound.*
>
> **—ALVIN LEE**

The Band

AUGUST 17, 1969

SET LIST

Chest Fever / Don't Do It / Tears of Rage / We Can Talk / Long Black Veil /

Don't You Tell Henry / Ain't No More Cane on the Brazos / This Wheel's on Fire /

I Shall Be Released / The Weight / Loving You Is Sweeter than Ever

THE BAND STARTED AS THE backing group of rockabilly artist Ronnie Hawkins. They split from him in 1964, and one year later, they were backing Bob Dylan. They relocated with him to Saugerties, New York, and in 1967 they recorded the songs that would eventually see release as Dylan's *The Basement Tapes*.

The following year, they dubbed themselves the Band and released *Music from Big Pink*. They would go on to release many albums that were well received, but that one is generally regarded as their masterpiece.

Containing their best-known song, "The Weight," the album was a revelation to many who heard it. It caused a seismic shift in the musical landscape, with many groups abandoning long-form jams and embracing folk-tinged songwriting. This included guitar hero Eric Clapton, whose time in the supergroup Cream was coming to a bitter and ugly end.

"I was given an acetate of *Big Pink* back in England and it shook me to the core," he said in 2017, according to CBC. "I was in Cream at the time with already the notion that it wasn't going in the right direction, and I thought, well this is what it is. I knew who Robbie Robertson was, but I didn't realize that was their group. I thought they just appeared. I thought they were all from the Mississippi Delta."

Clapton said that he was so taken with what the Band was doing that he went to visit them at their home in the town of Woodstock to play with them, and he found that they were operating on a completely different plane than he was.

"I thought, well, are we going to jam?" Clapton said. "They said, 'We don't jam, we write songs and play the songs.'...I thought, my God, these guys are real serious."

Despite having only one album to their credit, the Band was invited to perform at

Woodstock, and took the stage at ten o'clock on Sunday night. By that point, the grounds had endured over forty-eight hours of punishment, both from the elements and from the thousands of people who had taken up temporary residence in the mud.

> *We played a slow, haunting set of mountain music.... We did songs like "Long Black Veil" and "The Weight," and everything had a bit of reverence to it. Even the faster songs sounded almost religious.*
>
> —ROBBIE ROBERTSON

In his 1993 memoir, *This Wheel's on Fire: Levon Helm and the Story of The Band*, Band drummer and singer Levon Helm said that the wear and tear was easy to see.

"You kind of felt you were going into a war," he wrote. "There weren't any dressing rooms because they'd been turned into emergency clinics....The crowd was real tired and a little unhealthy."

Guitarist Robbie Robertson told *Rolling Stone* in 1989 that the audience being in the state that Helm described made them unsure of what kind of crowd they were facing. "After three days of people being hammered by weather and music, it was hard to get a take on the mood," Robertson said.

Upon taking the stage, the group turned in a performance that may not have been ideal for a festival crowd, but seemed appropriate to the musicians.

"We played a slow, haunting set of mountain music....We did songs like 'Long Black Veil' and 'The Weight', and everything had a bit of reverence to it. Even the faster songs sounded almost religious," Robertson said.

Although Jefferson Airplane's Grace Slick has been publicly ambivalent about the entire Woodstock experience, she had only good things to say about the Band's performance, even if her recollection was that they came off a little strangely in person.

"In the hotel, a bunch of us were in the lobby and a group called the Band came in the lobby and walked single-file, all dressed in black," she told *Rolling Stone* in 2014. "Didn't say anything to anybody and went straight back to the back of the hotel. We were all looking at them, like, 'Wow, that's weird! That's not especially friendly!' Boy, they were good, though."

Footage of the Band did not make it into the *Woodstock* documentary, or onto the soundtrack album, but it didn't matter. They were embraced by critics, musicians, and fans alike and rapidly became an internationally popular act. They even appeared on the cover of *Time* magazine in January 1970, just five months after performing at Woodstock.

After seven whirlwind years, they retired from touring. They held a star-studded farewell

The Band performing "a slow, haunting set of mountain music." (l-r: Guitarist and vocalist Robbie Robertson, singer and drummer Levon Helm, and bassist Rick Danko)

concert in November 1976, which featured such guests as Joni Mitchell, Neil Young, and Bob Dylan, and filmed it. Released in 1978 as *The Last Waltz*, the concert movie was directed by Martin Scorsese, who had worked on the *Woodstock* documentary as an editor, fittingly.

The Last Waltz is itself a convincing document of the hippie utopianism of the 1960s giving way to the bleary-eyed Quaalude hangover of the 1970s. According to the *San Francisco Chronicle*, close-up shots of Neil Young had to be "doctored in post-production" to remove visible evidence

of cocaine from the tip of his nose. If anyone needed proof that the party was over, this was it.

In the 1980s, the Band resumed touring, without Robbie Robertson. In 1986, keyboard player Richard Manuel committed suicide while the band was on tour, after years of struggling with drug and alcohol addiction. In 1999, bassist Rick Danko died, leading the group to break up once and for all.

Drummer Levon Helm died of cancer in 2012. As of this writing, only Garth Hudson and Robbie Robertson remain of the group that performed at Woodstock on August 17. ◆

Johnny Winter

AUGUST 17, 1969

WOODSTOCK MAY HAVE BEEN cursed with a lack of food and an unfortunate toilet situation, but one thing was in abundant supply—electric guitar players. One of the many who performed that weekend was Johnny Winter.

According to *Ultimate Classic Rock*, he was signed by Columbia Records in 1968 and given a $600,000 advance, which was then the largest ever given to a recording artist, and three times as much as the amount given to Led Zeppelin, which had itself broken records.

His self-titled Columbia debut came out in April 1969, and it contained nine tracks of gritty, down-and-dirty, electrified Texas blues, with zero varnish whatsoever. It was the real thing.

It featured the services of his younger brother, keyboard player Edgar Winter, and blues legend Willie Dixon even appeared on acoustic bass. Winter acted as his own producer, and it was clear from the first notes of side one that Johnny Winter knew exactly what he was doing.

Anyone familiar with his records knew what they were in for when he went onstage at Woodstock at midnight. He played cuts from his Columbia debut, such as "Leland Mississippi Blues" and "Mean Mistreater," and featured his brother Edgar on three songs, "I Can't Stand It," "Tobacco Road," and "Tell the Truth."

The set was not filmed, a decision that Winter attributed to his manager.

"Steve Paul didn't want us to be in the movie because he thought we wouldn't make any money," he said in his biography. "Woodstock had lost money up to that point and he thought it was gonna be a drag, so he didn't want us to be on it."

By then Winter had understood that this had been a major miscalculation, but of course it was impossible to do anything about it.

Guitarist Johnny Winter, who was then the recipient of the largest advance ever given to a recording artist by a record company.

"It helped a lot of people's careers," Winter said. "I wish I could have been in it. Later on, [Steve Paul] admitted he fucked up."

Winter released his next album, *Second Winter*, just two months after Woodstock, and kept touring and recording in the new decade. In the late 1970s, Chess Records shut down, leaving Muddy Waters without a label. Winter brought him into the studio and produced *Hard Again*, *I'm Ready*, and *King Bee* for the celebrated bluesman. These albums gave Waters's career a late-in-the-game commercial boost and allowed Winter the opportunity to lend a hand to a beloved idol.

Winter was comfortable with the fact that he was no matinee idol. He said in his biography that according to rumors that he had heard, he was kept out of the *Woodstock* documentary not just because of his manager, but because of the film's director, Michael Wadleigh.

"I heard the filmmaker said he thought the act was too strange," he said. "I don't know if that's true, but I heard that. The whole thing was full of strangeness—that's what Woodstock was all about—strange people."

Winter remained active, recording and touring, right up until his death in 2014 at age seventy. ◆

Blood, Sweat & Tears

AUGUST 17, 1969

BLOOD, SWEAT & TEARS WAS FORMED in 1967 by multi-instrumentalist Al Kooper. He left after the recording of their debut album due to "creative differences."

His departure could have been fatal to the band, but instead they drafted Canadian singer David Clayton-Thomas, who sang on their self-titled second album, and everything fell into place. When they went onstage at Woodstock at one-thirty on Monday morning, they had the number one album in the country.

On their way there, they were somewhat in the dark about the situation they were about to walk into.

"It was just another gig for us on the tour," Clayton-Thomas said. "We had landed at LaGuardia Airport and found out that the highway was closed from Albany to Long Island,

and then we literally sat at the airport for eight some-odd hours before they sent special buses for us, and they couldn't even get us close. We were actually flown in by National Guard helicopters."

When they touched down, Clayton-Thomas said that he saw several fellow Canadian musicians who, like him, had been complete unknowns just one year earlier.

"The Band was there, and they were old friends of mine," he said. "There we were at the largest concert in history, and a year ago we were playing bars on Yonge Street in Toronto."

Despite Woodstock's reputation as a peaceful event, he said that the mood between the groups' managers and the event's promoters was far less serene.

"There was no money because nobody was buying tickets," he said. "The managers and promoters were all huddled in a trailer, all screaming and arguing with each other, I think they were the only ones in the whole place screaming and yelling, and they were going on about, 'Who is going to get paid for this?'"

The promoters have said that every artist who performed was eventually paid, even if it took years to pay them. Clayton-Thomas said that to his knowledge, Blood, Sweat & Tears was never paid for its performance at Woodstock. However, he said that the appearance did so much to increase their visibility that not getting paid for a single night on the tour was irrelevant.

"We were a New York [City] band, and everybody in New York knew us, but everyone came to Woodstock from all over the country," he said. "So people saw us who normally would not have seen us. It certainly got us known for people who wouldn't normally see us."

He said that he wished that more people could have seen the performance. Specifically, movie audiences.

"Oh, we did a hell of a set," he said. "We were fired up! We did a great set."

Sadly, nobody but the Woodstock audience saw it. Concerning the decision to keep Blood, Sweat & Tears out of the movie, Clayton-Thomas said that their manager was responsible for that.

"I think it was the Band went on right before us, or right after us, I don't know, and Albert Grossman, their manager, made a big deal about the cameras being off because they weren't being paid," he said. "Then we went on and the cameras went on and they filmed our opening tune, and then our manager jumped onstage and said, 'I want the cameras turned off!', and so for the sake of one night's pay, they cut us out of history."

While he would have liked it if Blood, Sweat & Tears had been in the documentary, he doesn't hold grudges. He even came to the defense of the manager whose decision it was to stop filming.

"The managers are just doing their job, you know," he said. "They had airfares to pay, and a band to pay, and everything else."

Finally, he added that the Woodstock audience was more like today's music audiences than many people may realize, in at least one important respect.

Blood, Sweat & Tears singer David Clayton-Thomas at "just another gig for us on the tour."

"The fans so loved the music, they broke down the fences and didn't buy tickets," he said. "And the result of that, of course, was the promoters went [broke] and none of the acts got paid. Well, very few got paid. And if you fast-forward fifty years, the same thing is kind of going on now, that the fans think the music should be free, and they're streaming it on Spotify and whatnot. The result is the record companies are going bankrupt and the artists aren't getting paid again. It's trickle-down economics, isn't it?" ◆

Crosby, Stills, Nash & Young

AUGUST 17, 1969

SET LIST

Suite: Judy Blue Eyes / Blackbird /

Helplessly Hoping / Guinevere /

Marrakesh Express / 4 + 20 /

Mr. Soul / I'm Wonderin' / You Don't

Have to Cry / Pre-Road Downs /

Long Time Gone / Bluebird Revisited /

Sea of Madness / Wooden Ships / Find

the Cost of Freedom / 49 Bye-Byes

CROSBY, STILLS, NASH & YOUNG went onstage at Woodstock at three o'clock on Monday morning, August 18. Actually, Crosby, Stills & Nash did.

It's complicated.

At first, the group consisted of David Crosby of the Byrds, Stephen Stills of Buffalo Springfield, and Graham Nash of the Hollies. The three met at Joni Mitchell's house in Laurel Canyon when Crosby and Stills were no longer in their previous bands and Nash was getting fed up with his own.

They signed to Atlantic Records, and their self-titled debut was released in May 1969.

However, a problem arose. Stills had performed much of the instrumentation on the record, so another musician would have to be added to the lineup to replicate the material onstage. Atlantic Records president Ahmet Ertegun suggested Neil Young, Stills's former Buffalo Springfield bandmate.

Young's relationship with Stills has been described as rocky on many occasions, but the new quartet's contract allowed Young to continue his emerging solo career, so there was an escape hatch if needed. Besides, Crosby said that Young was interested in the group only as a catalyst for his own solo career.

"Neil didn't think [Crosby, Stills, Nash & Young] was a group," Crosby told *Vanity Fair*. "For him, it was a stepping-stone. He was always headed for a solo career; we were a way to get there."

Crosby, Stills, Nash & Young played their first-ever date at Chicago's Auditorium Theater on August 16, 1969. Then they went on to play their second-ever date, which was Woodstock. Chip Monck's twelve-year-old daughter was put in charge of keeping tabs on Stills.

He said that when Stills went to lie down before the performance, he saw something that he was probably not supposed to see.

"When he hopped into bed, his works fell out of his pocket," Monck said.

While this would be an alarming sight for many, Monck looked on the bright side.

"He just slipped them in between the mattress and the box springs, and that meant that Stephen was on the way to some sort of sanity."

Despite her youth and likely lack of experience babysitting rock stars, Monck's daughter did her job, and her charge made it onstage to join the rest of the group.

"This is only the second time we've performed in front of people," Stills said at the beginning of the performance. "We're scared shitless."

The set was split into acoustic and electric sections. The acoustic set opened with "Suite: Judy Blue Eyes" and consisted mainly of songs from the trio's debut. Neil Young emerged from the wings for the electric set.

According to his biography, *Shakey*, Young hated the group's performance, and he laid the blame on the movie cameras.

"We played fuckin' awful," he said. "I could see everybody changing their performances for the fuckin' camera and I thought that was bullshit."

He added that he refused to allow himself to be filmed, which is why only Crosby, Stills & Nash appeared in the *Woodstock* documentary, and he didn't.

"I wouldn't let them film me, that's why I'm not in the movie," he said. "I said, 'One of you fuckin' guys comes near me and I'm gonna fuckin' hit you with my guitar.'"

Half a century later, Michael Lang praised the group's performance, calling it the "best

Crosby, Stills, Nash & Young play their second show ever. (l-r. Graham Nash, David Crosby)

second show ever." Not everyone agreed.

"Crosby, Stills & Nash were terrible," said an attendee who identified as L. Broido. "Their harmonies were so off, I don't think they could hear themselves."

John Morris was not impressed either. "Crosby, Stills & Nash were out of tune the entire set," he said.

Seven months after the performance, Crosby, Stills, Nash & Young released *Déjà Vu*, which topped the charts upon release. According to the Recording Industry Association of America, it sold over eight million copies, making it the biggest-selling album not just for the group, but for each individual member as well.

In 2004, David Crosby told *Rolling Stone* about his favorite Woodstock memory.

"For me, the high point was us going out and singing 'Suite: Judy Blue Eyes' and getting all the way through it and not screwing up," he said. ◆

The Paul Butterfield Blues Band

AUGUST 17, 1969

SET LIST

Born Under a Bad Sign / No Amount
of Loving / Driftin' and Driftin' /
Morning Sunrise / All in a Day /
Love March / Everything's Gonna
Be Alright

PAUL BUTTERFIELD WAS A CHICAGO native. His family exposed him to blues music at an early age, and he quickly got hooked on it. Luckily, his father knew some of the local scene's most legendary musicians, which allowed the teenaged Butterfield to immerse himself in the music and culture, up close and personal.

"He was from the South Side," said his widow, Kathy Butterfield. "His dad was a pro bono lawyer who knew a lot of these guys already. I mean, Muddy Waters kind of adopted him."

He attended the University of Chicago, where he met guitarist Elvin Bishop. The pair hit it off, and before long, Butterfield had dropped out of college, intending to pursue music full time. The pair performed at local blues clubs, where eventually they were seen by producer Paul Rothchild. He convinced them to form a group with guitarist Mike Bloomfield, and they released their self-titled debut in 1965.

Drummer Sam Lay left afterward and was replaced by Billy Davenport, whose approach was jazzier than that of his predecessor. This changed their sound from that of a traditional Chicago blues band to one that merged the blues with the extended psychedelic jams of West Coast bands.

This shift in style was most evident on the title track of the group's second album, *East-West*. It clocked in at over thirteen minutes and took the blues into Eastern-tinged places where it had never gone before. That track, and the eight-minute interpretation of Nat Adderly's "Work Song," truly crossed lines and pushed boundaries.

Bloomfield left to form the Electric Flag, and the band's style began to drift away from psychedelic jams and toward a horn-oriented R&B sound. By August 1969, Paul Butterfield was the only original member of the band left, but that was beside the point. The group that performed at Woodstock consisted of top-flight musicians, including Grammy-winning saxophonist David Sanborn, and Kathy Butterfield said that her husband was thrilled to play with all of them.

"They were great musicians," she said. "He had a great horn section—Gene Dinwiddie,

LEFT: The Paul Butterfield Blues Band performing in the woods outside Paul and Kathy Butterfield's house in the town of Woodstock. RIGHT: The Paul Butterfield Blues Band in Paul and Kathy Butterfield's backyard. Paul Butterfield's shirt was made for him by Kathy. (l-r: Buzz Feiten, David Sanborn, Paul Butterfield, Gene Dinwiddie, Keith Johnson, Phillip Wilson, Steve Madeo; Rod Hicks on the ground; not pictured, saxophone player Trevor Lawrence)

David Sanborn, Steve Madeo, and Keith Johnson—and Rod Hicks was a fabulous bass player, and Phillip Wilson was a great drummer, and Buzzy Feiten was a really good guitar player."

The group didn't take the stage until six o'clock in the morning on Monday. Despite going on many hours later than intended, Kathy Butterfield said that both the group and the audience took their unusual set time for the happy accident that it was.

"It was kind of cool to play to the sunrise and have people still be so enthusiastic," she said. She also added that even if her husband had been peeved about any aspect of the appearance, you never would have heard about it from him, or from anyone he played with.

"Paul was just such a pro," she said. "All the people from that era, they were hard-working people. They were union musicians with a work ethic."

The group produced one more album, 1971's *Sometimes I Just Feel Like Smilin'*, and then broke up. Butterfield remained an active touring and recording musician right up until his death from a drug overdose in 1987. But for all the great music that he made during all those post-Woodstock years, Kathy Butterfield said that she still holds a particular fondness for the 1960s.

"It was a great time and after that, Jimi and Janis were gone, and later Paul," she said. "It was the highlight. It was the apex of a lot of the feeling of togetherness, not just because it was Woodstock. It was that time. We were all friends and all working the same places, the Fillmore, the festivals, the this, the that, and it was a good group of people who knew each other…I'm sorry everybody isn't still around." ◆

Sha Na Na

AUGUST 17, 1969

OF ALL THE ARTISTS WHO PERFORMED at Woodstock, the most anachronistic had to be Sha Na Na. Wearing leather jackets, gold lamé, and pompadours worthy of Arthur Fonzarelli, they performed fifties doo wop in an act that was equal parts homage and parody, and it had to be a bizarre sight on a sleep-deprived Monday morning as the LSD was wearing off.

"We were very much an anomaly," original guitarist Elliott Cahn said. "Audiences just adored us, for whatever reason… It evolved very 'word-of-mouth'-ish. They told their friends."

It wasn't just the audiences who felt that way.

"The musicians that we played with loved us," he said. "Janis, Jimi liked us, the guys in the Dead liked us, Keith Moon became our pal. We met him at the Reading Festival, in England, and he ended up flying over to New York to emcee a show of ours at Carnegie Hall."

Cahn conceded that their act was unlike everything else that weekend, but he said that it wasn't a big deal back then.

"Music in the late sixties, early seventies, was nowhere near so segmented as it is now," he said. "Many different genres could play together on the same bill, and the audience was very tolerant of things that were sort of outside their wheelhouse. Look at the bills for some of Bill Graham's shows, starting around 1967 or so, you'll see groupings of artists that just never would happen now."

Cahn had just turned twenty-one at the time of Woodstock. He spent much of the time before his band's performance gawking in doe-eyed wonder at what was going on around him. That wasn't limited to the festival grounds, either—when he and the group arrived at their hotel, there was an entire contingent of Hell's Angels there.

"There was a very straitlaced wedding going on there that day, that had been planned long before the Woodstock festival had come," he said. "I remember that the [Hell's] Angels all decided that they should kiss the bride. All of them."

Cahn may have been young, but he wasn't so green that he couldn't tell that conditions at the festival site were dire the moment he got there.

"The whole place smelled really bad," he said. "It smelled like a combination of mud and shit. But the fact that 400,000 people could be in an environment like that and generally be so euphoric is pretty extraordinary."

He added that at the time, he had no idea that he was performing at a festival that people would remember for the next fifty years.

"I had absolutely no sense of the significance that the event was going to end up having," he said. "It was just a big music festival, with a lot of terrific artists playing there, and an opportunity for my little, bitty, brand-new band to play for hundreds of thousands of people."

The group went on much later than originally scheduled. John Morris explained that this was so the more famous Paul Butterfield Blues Band could go on first. It ultimately played in the unknown doo-wop group's favor.

"Sha Na Na started to play their set when the sun was coming up, and they played the best set of their lives, and gave them a career that lasted years," he said. "They just went out and slayed them."

The group went on to massive success after Woodstock, eventually earning their own syndicated television show in 1977. More than forty members have passed through their ranks since then, but they're still together, which is more than you can say for a lot of the bigger bands that performed that weekend.

Cahn said that in his opinion, the festival signaled the end of the hippie movement's

Sha Na Na in 1969. "That's me sitting on the sidewalk in the lower left-hand corner," said original guitarist Elliott Cahn. "For your amusement, included in this crew of scary-looking derelicts are three future lawyers, two future medical doctors, and four future university professors."

cultural dominance. One need look no further than the Altamont festival to see his point.

"I think that the notion of 'peace and love' had crested," he said. "When you have things poorly planned, there are a number of ways it can go. It can go to the glorious, the way it was at Woodstock, or it can go to the just horrendous, the way it did at Altamont."

Cahn left Sha Na Na in 1973, but he stayed in the music business, eventually going into artist management. Ironically, he went on to manage Green Day, who performed at Woodstock '94. He added a postscript for anyone who doubted that Woodstock had been culturally significant.

"I've got two daughters, and they both saw the *Woodstock* movie in their seventh-grade American History class," he said. ◆

Jimi Hendrix

AUGUST 17, 1969

WHEN JIMI HENDRIX ACCEPTED THE OFFER TO headline Woodstock, taking the stage at nine o'clock on Monday morning was probably not what he had in mind. But after hours of rain delays, technical delays, and other problems, that's exactly what happened, so when the rest of the world was starting its workweek with coffee and doughnuts, he was bringing the festival to a close.

Hendrix's career was in a state of flux at the time. The Jimi Hendrix Experience, the power trio that he led when he became a superstar, had fractured, and bassist Noel Redding had left the group.

Rather than simply replace him with another bassist, Hendrix expanded the lineup and changed the group's name. He retained drummer Mitch Mitchell from the Experience and enlisted bassist Billy Cox, a friend from his days in the armed forces.

He then added guitarist Larry Lee and percussionists Juma Sultan and Jerry Velez to the lineup, dubbing the new group Gypsy Sun and Rainbows.

Despite his status as the headliner, most of the more than 400,000 people who had been there the past three days were not there to see Jimi Hendrix.

> *I didn't know Jimi was going to play "The Star-Spangled Banner." I played the first few notes and then just stopped and let him play.*
>
> —BILLY COX

"Jimi Hendrix played to almost no one," said Elliott Cahn of Sha Na Na. "I mean, ten thousand, fifteen thousand people, twenty thousand people, which is a fairly big crowd, but over several acres of land, so it looked like playing to almost no one."

The set consisted of such fan favorites as "Foxey Lady" and "Purple Haze," and new material that had not yet been recorded, such as "Jam Back at the House" and "Izabella." Most of the people who had stayed for the entire festival were glad that they did.

"I remember watching Jimi Hendrix, just in awe," said attendee Marla Argintar. "I mean he was amazing."

As the set drew to a close, the band played "Voodoo Child (Slight Return)." The guitarist told the audience that they could leave if they wanted to, because the group was "just jamming."

Those who left missed his screeching, explosive, feedback-soaked rendition of "The Star-Spangled Banner." That few minutes of music not only embodied what the end of three days of rain, mud, and LSD felt like, but served as a fitting close to the entire turbulent decade. It's not an exaggeration to say that it was a moment that defined the 1960s, along with the Martin Luther King, Jr. assassination, the Kennedy assassinations, and the moon landing.

"The Star-Spangled Banner" led directly into a ragged, undisciplined version of "Purple Haze," his best-known song, which led to a solo improvisation, and finally a full band piece. It was untitled at the time, but it would eventually be called "Villanova Junction." It was a slow, mournful dirge that was the perfect soundtrack for the concert's last attendees, who were trudging through the mud, utterly spent, to get back to the lives that they had abandoned days ago.

He performed an encore, "Hey Joe," but it was superfluous. He had already said in ten or fifteen minutes of music everything that could be said about the state of the nation, the culture, and the three days that had just gone by. Bassist Billy Cox told the *Guardian* in 2012 that he didn't even know it was going to happen.

"I didn't know Jimi was going to play 'The Star-Spangled Banner'," he said. "I played the first few notes and then just stopped and let him play."

After the festival, Gypsy Sun and Rainbows played a handful of gigs, including an appearance on *The Dick Cavett Show*, and then they broke up, less than a month after Woodstock. He and Cox enlisted drummer Buddy Miles and recorded a series of concerts at the Fillmore East, which resulted in the *Band of Gypsys* album, released in March 1970.

Jimi Hendrix would not release another album in his lifetime. He died in London at the age of twenty-seven on September 18, 1970. The autopsy found that he had choked to death on his own vomit while unconscious from sleeping pills.

According to the book *Ultimate Hendrix: An Illustrated Encyclopedia of Live Concerts and Sessions*, his girlfriend at the time, Monika Dannemann, said that he had taken nine of her Vesparax sleeping pills—eighteen times the recommended dosage.

Fans didn't have much time to recover from the news when they were dealt another blow. Janis Joplin's death from a heroin overdose—also at twenty-seven—came just sixteen days after Hendrix's passing, robbing the world of two immense talents who had played to hundreds of thousands just one year earlier. ◆

On Monday morning at nine o'clock, while most people were just pulling in to work, Jimi Hendrix closes out the Woodstock Music and Art Fair. Nobody who heard his rendition of "The Star-Spangled Banner" was ever the same again.

ENDINGS

We chose to drop flowers from helicopters. We chose to announce that we're all in this together and that the world was watching. We took that path every time when there was a fork in the road. And so, I think what we did was say to the people in the audience, "We're all part of this community and we, and one word that we can take, is loving and supporting each other." So that's the one—are you? And nobody wanted to say, "No, I'm not."

—JOEL ROSENMAN

Garbage

When Woodstock was over, a lot of garbage was left behind. While the festival was in progress, the glut of traffic made service by sanitation trucks impossible, which meant that there was no way to deal with the garbage until it was over. By then, the amount left behind was alarming.

"The place looked like the old Civil War photographs," said John Morris. "I walked the entire site looking for anybody who was hurt or injured or even worse, and didn't find anybody, thank God."

> ## I felt sorry for the guy that had to clean it up.
>
> —MARLA ARGINTAR

Attendee Marla Argintar said that it was impossible not to leave trash behind.

"There certainly weren't enough trash cans for people," she said. "You did the best you could. I mean, these people were not pigs."

In 2011, Shawn Amos of the *Huffington Post* detailed the numbers behind the garbage.

"Over six hundred acres of garbage was left behind on Max Yasgur's farm," Amos wrote. "It took over four hundred volunteers and one hundred thousand dollars to remove it all. A huge hole was dug to bury shoes, tents, bottles, and other debris. The garbage filled the hole and created a pile of trash that was set on fire, burning for days."

The Hog Farm collective had a flight to get to, so they were unable to take part in the cleanup. Wavy Gravy characterized this as "heartbreaking," but he believed in the people who were doing it instead of them.

"The task was to return venues to better shape than they were when we took them over in the first place," he said. "We saw that the people staying behind were prepared to go the distance."

A team managed by technical director Chris Langhart performed the cleanup. It was a long, unglamorous job, and some people just didn't stick around for it.

"Everybody just left," Langhart said. "They'd arranged for New York Carting or one of those giant outfits with big garbage trucks to come, and they had a lot of stuff put in bags. There were also a lot of piles of muddy blankets, stuff left from the rainstorm that were just all over the place."

He had the services of a crew for two weeks, which he paid for out of his own pocket. They would pick up refuse and put it in heaps, which the garbage trucks would then come and take away.

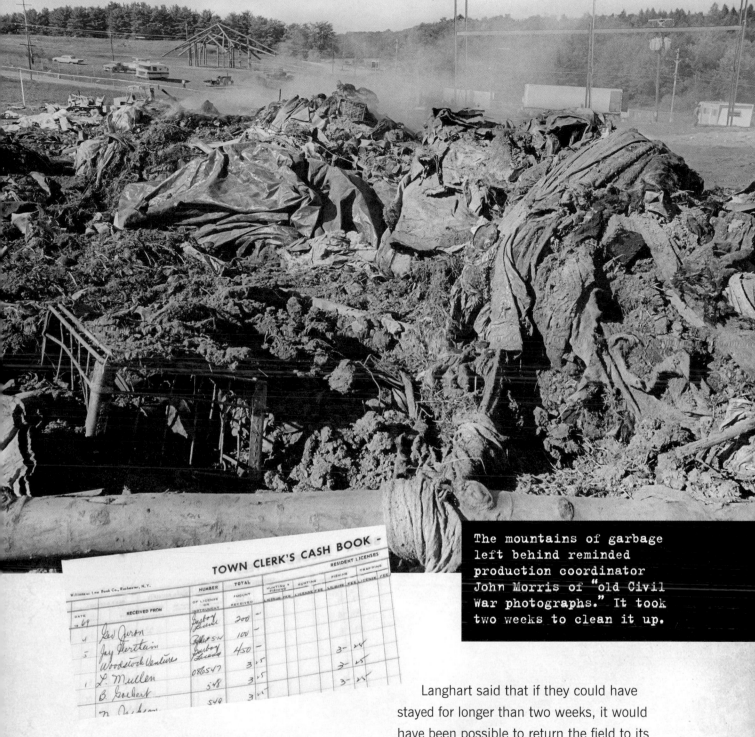

The mountains of garbage left behind reminded production coordinator John Morris of "old Civil War photographs." It took two weeks to clean it up.

TOWN CLERK'S CASH BOOK -

Langhart said that if they could have stayed for longer than two weeks, it would have been possible to return the field to its original, prefestival state. Sadly, they couldn't, so they didn't.

"I think I might have paid them twenty-five hundred dollars for everybody who worked on cleaning up," he said. "I went back in then later on and they made it good."

"We didn't get it back to pristine barn, no," he said. ◆

Coming Home

When the Woodstock audience started coming home, you could almost hear the cognoscenti in the news media licking their lips, salivating at the opportunity to declare the festival a disaster and the attendees a cross section of society's most depraved specimens.

They did not get their wish.

By all accounts, most had to concede that sure, these kids may have dressed funny and listened to crazy music, but they were not a menace to society.

On Monday, August 18, *The New York Times* had run an editorial critical of the festival, characterizing it as "an outrageous episode" and a mess of "colossal" proportions. The very next day, they ran a separate editorial that was the polar opposite of that one.

Woodstock, the new editorial said, was "essentially a phenomenon of innocence…they came, it seems, to enjoy their own society, to exult in a lifestyle that is its own declaration of independence."

Ted Lewis of the *New York Daily News* wrote that for the over 400,000 who had come to Woodstock, the festival was "a chance, perhaps, to express their emotional outlook on life which society fails to understand."

The larger cultural significance of Woodstock was a distant concern to those who had to find their way home from it. Audience member JoAnn Devitt had left early, but if she was hoping to beat the crowds and traffic, she was out of luck.

"We had to walk very far to find a way to get out, because there was so much backed-up traffic, and there were lots of people leaving," she said. "I actually got a sunburn while we were walking."

Attendee Jim Mesthene rode on the roof of a car.

"Probably not one of my wisest decisions," he said.

Having intimate knowledge of the area's back roads helped matters. You didn't get out quickly, but you could get out.

"We took back streets," said Joshua White, who left the festival after the first night. "It may have taken an hour to drive fifteen miles."

Audience member Vince Scarlata took one of his friends back to Cambridge, Massachusetts, when she got sick. Compared to the experiences that some festivalgoers had, he traveled in the lap of luxury.

"I flagged down a VW bus with Vermont plates," he said. "I said, 'You're going up to Vermont, give us a ride up to Cambridge,' and he drove us almost to the door."

An attendee identifying as L. Broido drove himself home.

"I was covered in mud," he said. "I hadn't slept in three days. I'd been taking psychedelics and I was talking to myself the whole way home."

Some of the people best positioned to comment on this weekend in Bethel didn't attend the festival. Richard Biccum, a Short Line bus driver who ferried people back to New York City's Port Authority terminal, told *The New York Times* that the concertgoers had been polite and orderly, despite their hippie garb.

"I'll haul kids any day rather than commuters," he said. Short Line dispatcher Reginald Dorsey agreed, saying that the passengers were "beautiful people" who caused no trouble.

Short Line employees had been so pleasantly surprised by the demeanor of the Woodstock audience that the company took out a half-page advertisement in *The New York Times*, quoting six drivers' comments about how pleased they were to serve the festival.

"We got to move thousands of kids to and from the festival," the advertisement read. "But better than that—they moved us. Deeply! Their generosity, patience, and good humor turned what might have been a difficult task into a revealing and enjoyable trip. We learned a lot about the young people around us. We love what we learned." ◆

Births and Deaths

Woodstock went down in history as a peaceful event, but there was still some loss of life that weekend. When it was over, the news reported two fatalities.

According to *The New York Times*, one unidentified attendee died of a heroin overdose. The other was Raymond Mizsak, a seventeen-year-old from New Jersey.

According to the *Trentonian News*, Miszak had come to the festival with his older sister, Kathleen. He made the unfortunate decision to set up his sleeping bag on a small knoll in the vicinity of a parked tractor.

At ten-thirty in the morning on Saturday, a driver got on the tractor and backed it up. The rear wheels of the water-tank trailer that it was towing rolled over him. According to *Rolling Stone*, he died just minutes before one of Woodstock Ventures' helicopters came to take him to the hospital.

John Morris disagreed with the news reports. While he remembered the incident involving Raymond Mizsak, he said that there were two other fatalities, not one, and they weren't drug overdoses.

"There were three deaths at Woodstock," he said. "One was [Mizsak]. The other two were Vietnam vets, who got really bad malaria attacks and were shipped out to the hospital by Bill Abruzzi, the doctor. The people at the hospital misdiagnosed them and left them alone in the field, and they both died."

Morris also addressed the longstanding myth about babies born at Woodstock.

"I have never seen any proof that there was a baby born at Woodstock," he said. "Now, it wouldn't surprise me honestly in the slightest. But I have no idea if it was, and nobody has ever introduced me to the baby, who's got to be fifty now."

There were, in fact, two births during the course of the festival, but they were not born on the actual festival grounds. Dr. Abruzzi told *The New York Times* that one was born at a hospital after the mother had been flown there by helicopter, and the other was born in a car stuck in standstill traffic on Route 17B. To this day, neither has ever been identified.

In 2009, Myron Gittell, author of the book *Woodstock '69: Three Days of Peace, Music, and Medical Care*, said that his own search for the legendary Woodstock baby—or babies—had turned up nothing. Still, he couldn't quite let the idea go entirely.

"Almost statistically, you'd think if there are a half-million people, and half of them were women, and 95 percent of them were of childbearing age, and fertile, and active," he said. "Just statistically, someone would have had to pop a baby." ◆

Dick Cavett

On August 19, 1969, *The Dick Cavett Show* aired, featuring several of the musicians who had just performed at Woodstock. Cavett was not part of the counterculture, but he was savvy enough to know that the people performing at Woodstock would make good television.

The guests included David Crosby and Stephen Stills, still wearing the muddy clothes in which they had performed, and Joni Mitchell, who had been invited to play Woodstock but turned it down on the advice of her manager.

Jefferson Airplane performed the song "We Can Be Together." The lyrics included the words "up against the wall motherfucker," and this was the first time anyone had uttered the word "fuck" on US television. Cavett knew it was coming, though, as he had been warned well ahead of time.

Chip Monck said that he met with the talk-show host in advance of the broadcast to bring him up to speed on who he was going to meet and what to expect, including some of the salty language found in the lyrics of Jefferson Airplane songs.

"I had been working with Dick for about a month before, at his home at the base of Long Island," Monck said. "And trying to explain to him who he was going to meet, who they were, what they felt, how much of a revolutionary spirit they would have, how polite, what language they would use."

Monck specifically made Cavett aware of the lyrics to "We Can Be Together," and he said that the talk-show host let it go.

"I warned him about 'up against the wall motherfucker', and other lyrics that might concern the network, and yet he let them through, which was great," Monck said. "He was extremely bright." ◆

Soundtrack Album

Woodstock: Music from the Original Soundtrack and More was a triple-record set released on Atlantic Records' Cotillion label in 1970. Its running time was two hours, a generous allotment for the LP days, but not nearly enough to feature every performer who had been there.

Still, for people who longed to reconnect with Woodstock, it did its job, providing a decent snapshot for those who hadn't been there.

The cover, taken from a photograph by Burk Uzzle of Magnum Photos, depicts two festivalgoers wrapped in a blanket. This became one of the most famous images from Woodstock.

The couple, Bobbi and Nick Ercoline, lived in nearby Middletown and had been dating for three months. They said that they had no knowledge that the photo was being taken, and they had had no plans to go to Woodstock in the first place.

"We were sitting on my porch that Friday night, listening to all the reports on whatever local station it was," Bobbi Ercoline said. "They said, the New York State Thruway is just clogged, do not come. If you plan on going, do not."

Rather than discourage the couple, the news made them realize that this was a once-in-a-lifetime event, and off they went. According to *Smithsonian* magazine, they were photographed in the early-morning hours of Sunday, August 17, as Jefferson Airplane performed.

"We were not identified until the twentieth anniversary," Bobbi Ercoline said. "Up until then, we were just an anonymous couple."

As for the music, not everything that appears on the soundtrack was performed at the festival. For instance, Crosby, Stills, Nash & Young's "Sea of Madness" was recorded at the Fillmore East in September 1969. And not everything on the record is music. Many stage announcements are included, such as the crowd chant of "no rain" and Chip Monck's warning about the brown acid.

Atlantic Records released *Woodstock 2* in 1971, a double album featuring artists from the first volume, as well as cuts by Melanie and Mountain, who had been left off the first volume. In 1994, Atlantic Records released *Woodstock: Three Days of Peace and Music*, which combined both existing soundtrack albums and added material by further artists, such as Janis Joplin, the Band, and Creedence Clearwater Revival.

In 2009, Rhino released *Woodstock 40 Years On: Back to Yasgur's Farm*, a six-CD set featuring material from every Woodstock performer, with the exception of Ten Years After, the Band, and the Keef Hartley Band. Despite

those omissions, this was the most complete overview of the music yet, as it included material by artists who had never been included on any Woodstock-related release, such as Sweetwater, Bert Sommer, and Quill.

As for the Ercolines, they've become minor celebrities, receiving everything from postcards to in-person visits from fans around the world. They welcome all of it, but they have mixed feelings about how music and imagery from the festival have been used in advertising.

"That's not in keeping with who we are and what actually happened there," Nick Ercoline said.

The couple added that they have never received any royalties or compensation for appearing in the photo, nor have they sought ownership of it, despite the likelihood that it could pad their bank account a bit. This is because they don't want it.

"We don't want to own that ourselves," Nick Ercoline said. "We want the experience to be owned by everybody." ◆

The Documentary

The *Woodstock* documentary was released in 1970 and was directed by Michael Wadleigh.

Many of the artists who performed don't appear in the original theatrical cut, which is a bone of contention for many of them. One of the bands left out was Canned Heat. The studio version of "Going up the Country" is in the film, but their performance isn't, and drummer Fito de la Parra was blunt in his assessment of why they were omitted.

"Typical corporate bullshit," he said. "[Warner Bros.] wanted to play the movie four times a day instead of three times a day. They made the movie shorter, and they took out a lot of acts that were not on their label."

Creedence Clearwater Revival was also left out of the movie, which bassist Stu Cook said was at bandmate John Fogerty's insistence.

"He was having a beef with the promoters over the pay, and I think he got an attitude and said, 'Well you know we're not going to be in the film,'" Cook said.

While many high-profile acts were cut from the movie, Sha Na Na was left in, despite the fact that Woodstock was the eighth profes-sional performance of their entire history.

"What I heard was that they started focus grouping the film, with the intention that we were going to get thrown out of it, and that our part went over particularly well with the focus groups," said guitarist Elliott Cahn. "So, that's why we got left in."

What nobody disputes is the quality of the movie.

"The movie was everything," Wavy Gravy said. "And great people were working on it too. Michael Wadleigh was a genius."

Andy Paley, who was sixteen, said that the documentary shows how straitlaced the Woodstock audience actually was.

"If you really look at that crowd, there's a shitload of guys with short hair and glasses, like pocket protectors and stuff like that," he said.

The documentary earned fifty million dollars at the box office, which allowed Woodstock Ventures to get out of debt eventually. Artie Kornfeld said that he was able to convince Warner Bros. to make the eleventh-hour deal for the movie only by playing up its potential to capture a unique disaster.

"I said, 'Well, what if something happens, and the towers fall down and two hundred kids die, you're going to have another *Titanic*, only a rock and roll *Titanic*'," he said. "We all started laughing and then we sat there for fifteen hours with just an empty pad, and we wrote out the movie deal between Warner Bros. and Woodstock Ventures. The deal I made was 50 percent of the gross, minus negative cost."

As part of the deal, Lang and Kornfeld gave up their share of the rights. Kornfeld said this cost the two of them about thirty million dollars.

"I just wanted the movie to come out so the kids in the future could see this miracle that happened," he said.

In 1994, a twenty-fifth-anniversary director's cut was released featuring forty minutes of new footage, including performances by Janis Joplin, Jefferson Airplane, and, yes, Canned Heat. It also contained a brief crowd shot that wasn't in the original, featuring attendee Gail Hayssen.

She said that forty years to the day after Woodstock, on August 15, 2009, she saw the DVD of the director's cut, not knowing she was in it. At roughly the hundred minute mark, she saw herself, thus ending a decades-long search for any evidence that she had been there. She said that it was important to her, because the festival had changed everything for her.

"The experience at Woodstock opened up a whole new vast way of living to me," she said. "I feel like it propelled me into my next stage of life, which was going into this whole hippie life and leaving New York and dropping out of high school and coming to California, living in communes and places all over. I would have to say that Woodstock had a very, very deep influence on that." ◆

RIGHT IN FRONT TO THE LEFT OF ME, A GUY CAME UP AND PAINTED, "WE ARE ONE." IT WAS PAINTED ACROSS THE FENCE RIGHT TO THE LEFT OF THE STAGE. RIGHT IN FRONT OF THE WOODSTOCK STAGE, AND I THOUGHT THAT THOSE THREE WORDS CAPTURED WHAT THAT EVENT WAS, AND I'VE NEVER FELT THAT KIND OF EXPERIENCE EVER AGAIN.

—Gail Hayssen

Index

Photo Credits

Principal photography © by Amalie R. Rothschild
Front endpapers, pages 1, 4, 5, 12, 13, 24, 25, 27, 33, 38-39 borders, 39 top right, 49, 55, 60-61 inset, 62, 63, 92, 96-97, 107, 111 top, 111 bottom, 128, 130-131, 136, 137, 140-141 inset, 144-145, 168, 169, 171, 173, 178 below left, 178 below right, 179, rear endpapers.

© ABC/Photofest, page 175.

© Gail Hayssen, pages 57 inset, 101, 105, 147.

© graphic stocker / Shutterstock, pages 58, 95, 139, 180.

© James T. Bonnell, page 186.

© Jonathan Charles Fox, pages 8, 9 below, 36 below, 37 below, 40 top, 40 middle left, 40 center, 40 middle right, 40 below left, 43 middle left, 43 center, 43 middle right, 43 below left, 43 below center, 43 below right.

© Jonathan Charles Fox / Town of Bethel Archives, White Lake, N.Y., pages 25 inset, 48 lower left, 48 lower right, 134, 135 top left, 135 top right, 171.

© Kathy Butterfield, page 161 left, 161 right.

© Mark A. Gore, mag_foto@mac.com, pages 2, 3, 40 below right, 44, 46-47 borders, 48-49 borders, 50, 57 background, 59, 60-61 borders, 86-87 borders, 90, 92-93 borders, 94, 96-97, 132-133 borders, 134-135 borders, 136-137 borders, 138, 140-141 borders, 170 borders, 172 borders, 174 borders, 176-177 borders.

© Mark A. Gore, mag_foto@mac.com, Courtesy Buddah Records page 71, Courtesy Elektra Records page 109, Courtesy Cotillion Records page 177.

© Roberta Becker, 36 top, 37 top right, pages 57 above and below, 94 top left, 94 top right, 94 bottom left, 94 bottom right, 172.

© Shutterstock/ThamKC, page 79.

©Andrea B. Stern / The Image Works, pages 19, 21.

©Dan Lenore / The Image Works, page 32 top, 93.

©Dan McCoy / The Image Works, pages 164-165.

©Elliot Landy / The Image Works, pages 7, 9 top, 15, 31, 41, 43-44 above, 65, 66-67, 69, 73, 75, 76, 81, 84, 85, 132, 143, 149, 150, 153, 155, 157.

©Henry Diltz / The Image Works, pages 121, 159.

©Jason Laure / The Image Works, pages 52, 103, 118, 124, 127.

©John Dominis / The Image Works, page 16.

©Lisa Law / The Image Works, pages 32 below, 87, 98-99.

©Mirrorpix / The Image Works, page 122.

© Peter Menzel / HIP / The Image Works, pages 167, 180.

©Raeanne Rubenstein / The Image Works, page 115.

©Roy Arenella / The Image Works, page 82.

©The Image Works Archives, 37 top left.

©Tom Miner / The Image Works, pages 86, 113.

©UPP / TopFoto / The Image Works, page 117.

© UPPA/Photoshot pages 88, 89, both photos.

© ZUMA Press, Inc. / Alamy Stock Photo, page 34.

Courtesy Everett Collection, page 11.

Courtesy of Joshua White, pages 22, 23, 26, 28, 29, 38 below left.

Parchment background, pages 45, 51, 53, 56, 88-89, 91, 132-133, 134-135, 136, 170-179, 182-186, 187, 188-191, 192.

Front Jacket: © Elliott Landy / The Image Works

Back Jacket: © Amalie R. Rothschild

Casewrap: © Amalie R. Rothschild

Resources

https://www.morrisonhotelgallery.com/search/Amalie-R_-Rothschild

http://tyedye-everything.com

mag_foto@mac.com

jonathanfoxemail@yahoo.com

Bibliography

Aletti, Vince. "Sly & the Family Stone: There's A Riot Goin' On," *Rolling Stone*, December 23, 1971.

AllMusic.com. (n.d.). Keef Hartley | Biography and History. Retrieved February 16, 2018, from https://www.allmusic.com/artist/keef-hartley-mn0000368783/biography.

Amos, Shawn. "The Long, Strange Trip of Woodstock Ventures," *Huffington Post*, September 13, 2009.

Ankeny, Jason. "Bill Graham Artist Biography," AllMusic.com.

Apple Music Classic Rock, Sampled: Mountain's "Long Red," Apple Music.

Associated Press. "Record Producer Slain; Police Charge His Wife," *The New York Times*, April 18, 1983.

Associated Press. "THE CITY; Wife Found Guilty In Pappalardi Case," *The New York Times*, September 22, 1983.

Attali, Jacques. *Noise: The Political Economy of Music*. Minneapolis: University of Minnesota Press, 1977.

Baez, Joan. *And A Voice to Sing With: A Memoir*. Summit Books, 1987.

Baltin, Steve. "Joan Baez Says She's Retiring From Touring, and Has Some Parting Words for the Left," *Variety*, October 13, 2017.

BBC News—Entertainment "Cocaine 'killed The Who star'." (2002, July 26). Retrieved February 16, 2018, from http://news.bbc.co.uk/2/hi/entertainment/2152761.stm.

Benzkofer, Stephan. "1970 Rock Concert at Grant Park Was a True Riot Fest," *Chicago Tribune*, July 25, 2015.

Blake, Mark. "What Really Happened the Night Keith Moon Died?" TeamRock.com, August 23, 2016.

Bleyer, Bill. "Road to Woodstock Runs Through Sunken Meadow," *Newsday*, August 8, 2009.

Bleyer, Bill. "Who Gets Credit for Legendary Woodstock Poster?" *Newsday*, August 8, 2009.

Bloom, Steve. "The Grateful Dead: A Chart History," *Billboard*, August 1, 2017.

Bodner, Brett. "Ten Facts You Didn't Know About Woodstock On The Anniversary Of The Iconic Outdoor Festival," *New York Daily News*, August 15, 2016.

Boyd, Joe. "A Mind-Bending Experience," *The Guardian*, January 4, 1997.

Brend, Mark. *American Troubadours: Groundbreaking Singer-Songwriters of the '60s*. Backbeat Books, 2001.

Browne, Ray B. *The Guide to United States Popular Culture*. Madison: University of Wisconsin Press, 2001.

Browne, David. "Grace Slick's Festival Memories: Fearing Orgies and Getting Lit," *Rolling Stone*, May 23, 2014.

Brustein, Joshua. "Woodstock in Newsprint," *The New York Times*, August 7, 2009.

Buckley, Peter. *The Rough Guide to Rock*. London: Rough Guides, 2003.

Byrd, David Edward. *Woodstock: An Aquarian Exposition, 1969*. David Edward Byrd, David-Edward-Byrd.com.

Cherie, C.M. "Musicians Pay Tribute to Cornish Folk Legend Clive Palmer from Penzance," *The Cornishman*, November 25, 2014.

Christgau, Robert. "The Incredible String Band," *Consumer Guide Reviews*, Robertchristgau.com.

Cobo, Leila. "Smooth" at 15: Carlos Santana and Rob Thomas Reflect on Their Billboard Hot 100 Smash," *Billboard*, June 27, 2014.

Collier, Barnard L. "Tired Rock Fans Begin Exodus," *The New York Times*, August 18, 1969.

Coulehan, Erin. "Richie Havens' Ashes Scattered at Woodstock," *Rolling Stone*, August 19, 2013.

Country Joe's Place. That Notorious Cheer, Countryjoe.com.

Dann, David. "The Mike Bloomfield Story," *Mike Bloomfield: An American Guitarist*, http://www.mikebloomfieldamericanmusic.com/.

DeRiso, Nick. "The Day Canned Heat Frontman Bob Hite Overdosed Between Sets," *Ultimate Classic Rock*, April 5, 2016.

DeRiso, Nick. "Who Talk About Woodstock's Disappointment and Explosive TV Appearance"— Exclusive Book Excerpt, Ultimateclassicrock.com, November 4, 2014.

Dufour, Jeff. "Woodstock Producer: Roy Rogers, Not Hendrix, Could Have Closed," *The Washington Examiner*, August 8, 2009.

Dumas, Timothy. "A Woodstock Moment – 40 Years Later," *Smithsonian Magazine*, August 2009.

Ellis-Petersen, Hannah. "Joe Cocker, Grammy-Winning Singer, Dies at Age of 70," *The Guardian*, December 22, 2014.

Evans, Mike. *Woodstock: Three Days that Rocked the World*. New York: Sterling, 2009.

Farber, Jim. "Joni-Come-Lately," *New York Daily News*, August 13, 1998.

Fisher, Marc. *Something in the Air: Radio, Rock, and the Revolution That Shaped a Generation*. New York: Random House, 2007.

Fornatale, Pete. *Back to the Garden: The Story of Woodstock*. New York: Touchstone, 2009.

Fusilli, Jim. "Woodstock's Forgotten Man," *Wall Street Journal*, August 6, 2009.

Garofoli, Joe. "Obama Riffs on Santana Tripping at Woodstock," *San Francisco Chronicle*, December 9, 2013.

Glass, Philip. "George Harrison, World-Music Catalyst and Great-Souled Man; Open to the Influence of Unfamiliar Cultures," *The New York Times*, December 9, 2001.

Graff, Gary. "Woodstock at 40: Promoter Michael Lang Interviewed," *Billboard*, July 31, 2009.

Graff, Gary. "Woodstock at 40: Where Are They Now?" *Billboard*, July 30, 2009.

Green, David B. "This Day in Jewish History 1973: The Farmer Who Defied His Neighbors and Hosted Woodstock Dies," *Haaretz*, February 9, 2016.

Greene, Andy. "Dazed and Confused: 10 Classic Drugged-Out Shows," *Rolling Stone*, June 6, 2013.

Greene, Andy. "Santana on Reuniting Classic Lineup, How to Fight Trump," *Rolling Stone*, May 19, 2016.

Greene, Andy. "The Band Play 'Tears of Rage' at Woodstock," *Rolling Stone*, November 26, 2013.

Grimes, William. "Cynthia Robinson, Sly and the Family Stone Trumpet Player, Dies at 71," *The New York Times*, November 26, 2015.

Guthrie, Arlo. "Karl Dallas, January 29 1931— June 21 2016," *The People's Daily Morning Star*, June 29, 2016.

Hennessy, Christina. "Woodstock Poster Designer's Paintings on Exhibit in Stamford," *The Stamford Advocate*, October 15, 2010.

Hillburn, Robert. "The Irony of Woodstock: The Celebration of the Age of Aquarius Was Also the Weekend the Music Turned into Money," *Los Angeles Times*, June 18, 1989.

Hodenfield, Jan. "After Woodstock: Money and Smiles, *Rolling Stone*, October 4, 1969.

Hodenfield, Jan. Woodstock: 'It Was Like Balling for the First Time,' *Rolling Stone*, September 20, 1969.

Hudson Valley 1 staff. "Former Councilman Steve Knight Dies," April 24, 2017. Retrieved February 16, 2018, from https://hudsonvalleyone.com/2013/01/27/former-councilman-steve-knight-dies/.

Huey, Steve. "Paul Butterfield Biography," Allmusic.com.

James, Gary. "Interview with John Sebastian of the Lovin' Spoonful," Classicbands.com, January 13, 2009.

Kahn, Victor. "In Memory of Bert Sommer," Bertsommer.com, 2004-2013.

Kamp, David. "Sly Stone's Higher Power," *Vanity Fair*, August 2007.

Kelly, Jack. "EMS at Woodstock," *Journal of Emergency Medical Services*, April 28, 2010.

Kinos-Goodin, Jesse. "That time Eric Clapton Auditioned for—and Was Rejected by—the Band," CBC, September 15, 2017, from https://www.cbc.ca/radio/q/blog/that-time-eric-clapton-auditioned-for-and-was-rejected-by-the-band-1.4289615.

Krajicek, David J. "Gail Collins, Infamous Lyricist Who Killed Husband Felix Pappalardi, Found Dead in Mexican Village," *New York Daily News*, February 22, 2014.

Kreps, Daniel. "Signe Anderson, Original Jefferson Airplane Singer, Dead at 74," *Rolling Stone*, January 31, 2016.

Lancashire Post. "Preston Drummer Who Played at Woodstock Dies Aged 67." December 1, 2011. Retrieved February 16, 2018, from https://www.lep.co.uk/whats-on/music/preston-drummer-who-played-at-woodstock-dies-aged-67-1-4020224.

Landau, Jon. "Creedence Clearwater Revival: Mardi Gras," *Rolling Stone*, May 26, 1976.

Littleproud, Brad. *Woodstock—Peace, Music & Memories*. Iola: Krause Publications, July 3, 2009.

Martin, Douglas. "Swami Satchidananda, Woodstock's Guru, Dies at 87," *New York Times*, August 21, 2002.

McDermott, John. *Ultimate Hendrix: An Illustrated Encyclopedia of Live Concerts and Sessions*. Milwaukee: Hal Leonard Corporation, 2009.

McDonough, James. *Shakey: Neil Young's Biography*. New York: Random House, 2002.

McQuiston, John T. "Abbie Hoffman, 60's Icon, Dies; Yippie Movement Founder Was 52," *The New York Times*, April 14, 1989.

Mitchell, Kevin M. "Parnelli Innovator Honoree, Father of Festival Sound," *Front of House Online*, September 2006.

Modzelewski, Joseph. "Traffic Uptight at Hippie Fest," *New York Daily News*, August 16, 1969.

Myers, Marc. "The Story Behind 'Darling Be Home Soon' by the Lovin' Spoonful's John Sebastian," *Wall Street Journal*, December 28, 2016.

Newspapers.com. "Alice's Restaurant Massacree," "Alice's Restaurant," "Arlo Guthrie." (n.d.). Retrieved February 16, 2018, from https://www.newspapers.com/clip/3747386/alices_restaurant_massacree/.

O'Mahony, John. "A Hodgepodge of Hash, Yoga and LSD," *The Guardian*, June 4, 2008.

Pareles, Jon. "Woodstock: A Moment of Muddy Grace," *The New York Times*, August 5, 2009.

Post Staff Report. "Funk Legend Sly Stone Homeless and Living in a Van in LA," *New York Post*, September 25, 2011.

Reiff, Corbin. "10 Facts You Probably Didn't Know About Johnny Winter," *Ultimate Classic Rock*, February 23, 2016.

Reiff, Corbin, "The Complicated, Generation-Defining History of Woodstock," *Ultimate Classic Rock*, August 15, 2014.

Reynolds, Susan. *Woodstock Revisited: 50 Far-Out, Groovy, Peace-Loving, Flashback-Inducing Stories From Those Who Were There*. Avon, MA: Adams Media, 2009.

Roberts, Jim. *How the Fender Bass Changed the World*. Backbeat Books, May 11, 2001.

Roberts, Randall. "Why Sly Stone Still Can't Collect Royalties from his Classic Songs," *Los Angeles Times*, December 12, 2015 .

Robinson, Lisa. "An Oral History of Laurel Canyon, the 60s and 70s Music Mecca," *Vanity Fair*, March 2015.

Rolling Stone. "Woodstock in 1969," (n.d.). Retrieved February 16, 2018, from https://web.archive.org/web/20070209163601/http://www.rollingstone.com/news/story/6085488/woodstock_in_1969.

Romm, Ethel. "Sex, Drugs, Rock 'N Roll in Redneck Country," *Huffington Post*, September 15, 2009.

Ruhlmann, William. "Ten Years After Artist Biography," AllMusic.com.

Salkin, Allen. "As Woodstock Turns 40, No Agreement on Tribute," *The New York Times*, May 8, 2009.

Sauer, Patrick. "Country Joe's Obscene Truths," *The New York Times*, October 10, 2017.

Selvin, Joel. "The Day the Music Lived / Rereleased 'Last Waltz' Documents Amazing Night in 1976 When Rock's Royalty Bid Farewell to the Band," *San Francisco Chronicle*, April 4, 2002.

Simpson, Dave. "How We Made: Michael Lang and Billy Cox on Woodstock," *The Guardian*, November 26, 2012.

Solomon, Deborah. "Just Folk," *The New York Times*, July 21, 2009.

Spiegel, Alison. "Peace, Love, and Granola: The Untold Story of the Food Shortage at Woodstock," *Huffington Post*, March 9, 2015.

The Trentonian. "Peace, Love, and the Hamilton Teenager Who Died at Woodstock," August 16, 2009. Retrieved February 16, 2018, from http://www.trentonian.com/article/TT/20090816/news/308169995.

Stephens, Brittney. "The Details of Jimi Hendrix's Death Are Still Pretty Frightening, Even 50 Years Later," MSN.com, January 9, 2017.

Sullivan, Mary Lou. *Raisin' Cain: The Wild and Raucous Story of Johnny Winter*, Backbeat Books, April 1, 2010.

Ten Years After. "The Classic Years," 1967–1968: The Beginning of a Great Rock'n'Roll Band: Ten Years After, Alvinlee.de.

The New York Times. "A Toilet Cleaner Loses Suit over 'Woodstock'," November 18, 1974. Retrieved February 16, 2018, from http://www.nytimes.com/1974/11/18/archives/a-toilet-cleaner-loses-suit-over-woodstock.html.

Tugend, Tom. "A Jewish Visit to Guthrie's Land," *The Jewish Journal*, December 2, 2004.

U.S. Department of Justice, Federal Bureau of Investigation. *Terrorism 2000/2001*, FBI.gov.

Unterberger, Richie. *Eight Miles High: Folk-rock's Flight from Haight-Ashbury to Woodstock*. Backbeat Books, 2003.

Unterberger, Richie. "Tim Hardin Artist Biography," AllMusic.com.

Varga, George. "Legendary Concert Promoter Bill Graham Died 25 Years Ago Today," *San Diego Union-Tribune*, October 25, 2016.

Waddell, Ray. "Grateful Dead Concerts Made $52 Million, Set Record for Biggest Music PPV Event Ever," *Billboard*, July 23, 2015.

Wales Online. "Paul Kantner Talks Woodstock, Jefferson Starship, and Smashed Cars," March 28, 2013. Retrieved February 16, 2018, from https://www.walesonline.co.uk/lifestyle/showbiz/paul-kantner-talks-woodstock-jefferson-2070790.

Weindling, Dick. *Decca Studios and Klooks Kleek: West Hampstead's Musical Heritage Remembered*. Stroud UK: The History Press, 2014.

Weisel, Al. "Ravi Shankar on His Pal George Harrison and 'Chants of India'," *Rolling Stone*, May 15, 1997.

Whitaker, Sterling. "John Fogerty Clarifies His Views on Creedence Clearwater Revival Reunion," *Ultimate Classic Rock*, May 26, 2013.

Woodstock Story. "Interview with Arnold Skolnick," (n.d.). Retrieved February 16, 2018, from http://www.woodstockstory.com/arnold-skolnick.html.

Yardley, William. "Alvin Lee, British Blues-Rock Guitarist, Dies at 68," *The New York Times*, March 6, 2013.

Zimmerman, Lee. "Happy Birthday, John Mayall!," *The Broward Palm Beach New Times*, November 29, 2011.

Acknowledgments

I'd like to thank the following people for helping me bring this book to life. Every contribution helped, no matter what it was, and I'm extremely grateful for all of it.

Thank you to Patricia Allen, Marla Argintar, Amanda Bennett, Roberta Becker, Patricia Biedinger, Constance Brinkley-Badgett, L. Broido, Ernie Brooks, Ashley Timberlake Brown, Connie Brown, Wendy Brynford-Jones, Pat Burns, Kathy Butterfield, Carol's Dream, Elliot Cahn, Nancy Cahn, Elise Caitlin, Emily Casey, Kathy Christopherson, Carol Clapp, David Clayton-Thomas, Winnie Co, Dan Cole, Stu Cook, Adolfo "Fito" de la Parra, Jack Deacy, JoAnn Devitt, Duke Devlin, George Douvris, Bobbi Ercoline, Nick Ercoline, Arlene Falcon, Brent Farmer, Dikko Faust, Darlene Fedun, Jonathan Charles Fox & Dharma the Wonder Dog, Carol Girard, Myron Gittell, Lorraine Goonan, Mark A. Gore, Sally Greenberg, Syed Haider, Bill Hanley, Gail Hayssen, Ira Heaps, Hectors, Stephen Hopkins, Roy Howard, Jeryl Abramson & Family, Dia Huizinga, Lisa Johnson, Richard Julio, Jennifer Jessica Justice, Colleen Kane, Jeffrey Karasik, Jim Killilea, Zoe Knight, Artie Kornfeld, Elliott Landy, Michael Lang, Chris Langhart, Wade Lawrence, Gene Lee, Anne Leighton, Nancy Leonard, Jim Lomax, Joan Lundbohm, Adrian Lyss, Sara Jane LaLiberté Mäki, Charlie Maloney, Sara Spolan Marricco, Alex Matsu, Philip Matsu, Chris McArdle, Kevin McDaniels, Jim Mesthene, Chip Monck, John Morris, Dan Mouer, the Museum at Bethel Woods, Mark Naftalin, the National Register, Roberta Nelson, Nancy Nevins, Betsy Nichols, Sue Owens, Andy Paley, Jonathan Paley, Heather Crist Paley, Daniel C. Parmenter, Christine Piwonka-Bernstein, Jennifer Powers, Megan Bencivenni Quinn, Lori Rami, Maureen Riley, Jahanara Romney, Jordan Romney, Joel Rosenman, Amalie R. Rothschild, Marc L. Rubinstein, Mary Ann Sabia, Melanie Safka, Vince Scarlata, Mel Schuit, scnyhistory.org, Drew Semon, Rita Sheehan, Sid Shigematsu, Charlotte Silverstein, Esther K. Smith, P.J. Soles, Dan Sorenson, Joanna Spencer, Ruth Spencer, Donna Spurlock, Don Stark, Meredith Stark, Kenneth Stephens, Kevin Stevens, Bonnie Stone, Pamela Stone, Inge Strack, Gerry Swislow, Larry Taylor, Skip Taylor, Julie Tesser, Paul Toscano, Marion Vassmer, Sarah-Maria Vischer-James, Ted Waddell, Brian Walker, Wavy Gravy, Don Weise, John Wenckelium, Joshua White, Steve Wise, Stuart Wolferman, Jerry Wolfert, woodstockpreservation.org, Lynne Yeamans and Mark Yessin.

I'd also like to give personal thanks to my parents, Albert and Joanna Bukszpan, my sister, Claudia Bukszpan Rutherford and my in-laws, Valborg Fletre Linn, Don Blanford and Hjordis-Linn Blanford.

Most of all, I'd like to thank my wife, Asia and my son, Roman. I couldn't do what I do without you. I love you both more than anything.